To Duke —

  May you too claim
all the promises He has
made to all of us.
        Love,
        Jeanne.
        Spring Retreat
        Windsor, Ontario,
          Canada
          1966

MAGNIFICENT PROMISE

*A Fresh View of the Beatitudes—
from the Cross*

MAGNIFICENT PROMISE

*A Fresh View of the Beatitudes—
from the Cross*

By

SHERWOOD ELIOT WIRT

Foreword by EUGENIA PRICE

MOODY PRESS

CHICAGO

TO

Faith McCain Wells

WHO SHOWED ME HIS FACE

Foreword

IT IS RARE when one finds writing of the caliber offered in this book. It is *very* rare in books about Jesus Christ.

Sherwood Wirt has done his subject justice. Not only in the strong, clean literary style, but in spiritual insights into the very heart of Christ, and what it means to be His follower.

Here one finds a lovely balance between the author's seeing and the expression of that sight.

If the old, stereotyped religious clichés have slipped over the reader's daily conscience until they no longer leave *any* impression, this book is required reading.

Jesus Christ will step from its pages, alive—out of the tomb forever, as He really *is*, stripped of antiquity, approaching the reader with the same great, open, eager heart that broke on Calvary for love of the whole human race.

EUGENIA PRICE

Preface

THE OPENING VERSES of the Sermon on the Mount, known as the Beatitudes, are sometimes taken to be simply descriptions of the "ideal" life, a life of good character and good conduct to which we should all aspire. Yet everything Jesus said was colored by His sense of personal mission on behalf of mankind, which issued ultimately in His vicarious sacrifice on the Cross. These pages seek to interpret the Beatitudes not so much as descriptions of the "ideal" life as of the "crucified" life. If the scholarly and homiletic approaches have been avoided, it is because the chapters were first conceived as meditations rather than as treatises or sermons.

This volume originally appeared under the title *The Cross on the Mountain,* and is now being reprinted by Moody Press through the kind interest and offices of the editor, Mr. Robert K. DeVries. It has been revised and some minor corrections have been made.

Many of the chapters were conceived while on "pastor's day off" hikes in the coast range hills of California. Those hours were among the richest of my life; no joy can compare with that which comes from a contemplation of the words of Jesus. I wish to thank Mr. Robert J. Cadigan for originally encouraging my entry on this study, and Mr. David Scott for editorial guidance. My prayer is that God will use the chapters not only to stimulate and challenge the reader but to bless him as well.

S. E. W.

Minneapolis, Minnesota

Contents

MAGNIFICENT
PROMISE

BLESSED ARE THE POOR IN SPIRIT:

FOR THEIRS IS THE KINGDOM OF HEAVEN.

1

Beyond the Rope's End

I

MANY OF US learned the words as children and grew up with them. They are lovely words with a comforting sound, words that seem to promise much and to exact little. How easily they roll off our tongues! As if we were saying, "If you are very polite, you will have an extra slice of cake with your ice cream," or, "If you get to work punctually at eight each morning, you will probably marry the boss's daughter and be taken into partnership."

When we examine our Beatitude more carefully, however, we begin to make important discoveries. We find that the words do not mean at all what we have supposed them to mean. When we study them in the light of the One who spoke them, it becomes evident that we cannot divorce the teachings of Jesus Christ from His

1

life. What He is actually doing is sending up a rocket in this verse to signal the direction to the Cross of Calvary. In doing so He is laying down a basic principle of the Kingdom of God.

What is poverty of spirit? Jesus does not in any sense suggest (for all the insinuations of such critics as Celsus and Nietzsche) that weakness is preferable to manliness. To be poor in spirit is not contrary to being high-spirited; rather it is the opposite of spiritual pride. Poverty of spirit means that the ground of our self-sufficiency has been removed from under us. It means that our resiliency is gone, that we have given up assuming that "everything is going to turn out all right." It is the cry of dereliction from the Cross: "My God, my God, why hast thou forsaken me?" It is the bitter sobbing of Mary in the garden. It is the heart upon its knees.

Jesus is telling us something we very much need to know: that there is no need for us to try to "save face" before God. In the things of the Spirit it is important to be honest and frank. One of the hardest things our Lord had to bear was the criticisms of those who were making capital of their churchmanship. Such persons desired their piety to be "seen of men." There is no pride like spiritual pride. No matter how great our evangelistic zeal or how arduous our labors in the church kitchen, we may claim no heavenly trophies for our attainments. As Christians we are aware that even these duties may develop into tumors to draw off the divine life seeking to flow into us; that the only spiritual progress really possible for us is toward the Cross, and that is toward spiritual poverty.

The secret of the Gospel's power is that it alone can deal adequately with the whole matter of pride and humility. It exposes the falsity of those who pretend to be spiritually rich. At the same time it undercuts the false humbleness of those who, like Dickens' famous Uriah Heep, use their obsequiousness as a vehicle to foster their pride. Christian humility is not merely modesty; it is the stark humiliation of Golgotha.

The more we concentrate our gaze on the Cross, the more clearly this Beatitude speaks to us. The way of the Cross is not a velvet carpet for a prince of the Church, nor is it a *Via Appia* for the triumphant conqueror. It is a poor way, an unfriendly and deserted way, soiled with blood, sweat, and tears. It is a way that breaks down even a man's spiritual vitality, and leaves him at the end of his tether. It leads not to self-realization but to self-sacrifice; to the wolves and the Roman execution squad. To walk this way is not to be filled with the Spirit but to be emptied by the Spirit.

When we have reached that crucifixion point—call it high or low—when we recognize that we are unprofitable servants, the divine blessing is released. How else could God work? He cannot fill our cups with the Water of Life until they have been drained of all other waters. That is why the blessed ones are those who are poor in spirit. It is their poverty, their insolvency, that gives them the capacity for taking on treasure. Who enjoys a meal when his stomach is already filled? "The righteous have no need of a physician." Until a man's hands are empty he cannot reach for the hand of God. There is only one way to the resurrection and that is by way of the Cross.

A day of penitence and sober reflection, therefore, could be the equinox of God's springtime in our lives. It was as he sat in dust and ashes that Job saw the Lord. What Christ is teaching us is more than a "principle of the Kingdom," it is the secret of life itself.

2

As soon as we seek to apply the principle in our daily walk, it becomes apparent that our first need to be "poor in spirit" is not in our relations with each other but—surprisingly enough—in our prayer life. All men are children of their times, and while we twentieth-century people are more conscious of the sin and tragedy of life, perhaps, than our forebears were, we are not aware of how our era is debasing prayer. Prayer has become a weapon in the cold war. It has been made a slide rule for financial investments. It has been invoked to avoid medical expenses and to heighten luxury. It has been made into an escape hatch for thwarted ambition. Many people have callously and blasphemously tried to manipulate God through prayer. They have sought to make a "science" of prayer, comparing it with electricity, speculating upon its "wave lengths" and "vibrations" and treating the Holy Spirit as if He were a kind of space-station transmitter.

Perhaps it is natural that in a century of exploitation and propaganda there is danger of prayer becoming a racket. Just as scientists have launched their fabricated moons in an effort to gain a purchase on space, so "religious" people are exporting prayer into the unknown in the hope of obtaining a favorable trade balance with Something Out There. More than one Organization Man, impressed by the popularity of religion, has sought greater efficiency for his business by inviting God to sit with his board of directors.

The question seems not to be, "What is God like?" or "How may I seek His face?" but simply, "How can I control Him?" Thus in addition to providing an inexpensive psychiatry, prayer becomes modern man's technique for outfoxing the hounds of his own materialism, and his insurance program against the wrath of God.

The Beatitude changes all this. It makes clear that our prayers are to begin neither with wishing nor with scheming. True prayer begins with nothing. "A broken and a contrite heart, O God, thou wilt not despise." (Psalm 51:17) It begins in Gethsemane with the words of Jesus, "Nevertheless, not my will, but thine." A missionary tells of visiting an Indian woman in the last stages of cholera. Her body was wasted and her breathing was labored, and he had only a few minutes. With great effort he taught her to repeat in the darkened room the beginning of the Twenty-third Psalm, "The—Lord —is—my—shepherd——I—shall—not—want." That is the beginning of prayer!

The very thought of trying to manipulate God is

profane, and should strike terror into the honest believer. Here surely it is true that the fear of the Lord is the beginning of wisdom. Such "praying" is always childish and self-answering, but it can be outgrown. The moment we give over our immature efforts to use the Almighty for our own ends, and begin to yearn for Him for His own sake, our boldness returns. When a man lifts up empty hands to God they become holy hands.

Because we spend so little actual time in prayer, we are tempted to look at it as a professional skill rather than simply a conversation with God. We even think it is performed at its best by professionals in proper garb. A corrective is needed here. Ezekiel once had a vision of wheels, but his wheels were not the leaders of the Church. Prayer is not ecclesiastical politicking. Today, as in the days of Moses, the mighty man of God may be a Church leader and he may not, but it is certain that if his prayer has prevailing power he is not a spiritual giant, he is a spiritual dwarf. He is the poor in spirit. Like Peter, he is "broke"—("silver and gold have I none")— that is, he is broken. As God cuts him down to grasshopper size, or to worm size, he discovers just how valuable are all his programs of pious affiliation.

Again, so many of us have come to feel that prayer, like the Christian life, is a moving passenger train that we ought to be aboard. We run and try to jump on, but through ineptness we fail to make the step. As in a nightmare we see that our efforts to cling are in vain, and we lose our grip. One by one we watch the cars pass us by. Other people find Jesus Christ, learn to pray, find vic-

6

tory in their lives, acquire a testimony, and move on, but we remain mute.

The prayers of others frequently frighten us, they are so artistically and fervently expressed; they fairly radiate joy and assurance. We become quite discouraged. Yet the one prayer that Jesus Christ honored above all others was the wail of a thieving tax collector: "God be merciful to me, a sinner." As Charles Spurgeon remarked from his London pulpit, "This publican had the soundest theology of any man in all England." He described himself as a sinner, and in the world of the Spirit what is a sinner? He is nothing. The New Testament was written not by men of spirit but by the Holy Spirit of God moving in men of nothing.

3

There are thousands of us who are able to discourse seemingly upon any subject, like the television experts, but at the moment of spoken prayer our jaws are frozen shut. Why? Is it because our sins rise up and condemn us? Is it because, after all, we do not really believe? Why do God's people become inarticulate and feel they cannot call upon Him? One of the commonest apologies, of course, is that one has not "come that far yet," one has not "moved along spiritually to the point" of prayer, one has not acquired sufficient skills to verbalize prayer.

Does prayer then require some sort of *expertise?* How much training is needed for a man to say, "Thank you, Lord!" or "Abba, Father," or "God be merciful to me, a sinner"? The Cross certainly does not suggest

7

that God requires polish and finesse from the men who approach Him. Humanly speaking, the crucifixion of Jesus Christ was the worst bungle in history, yet it accomplished our salvation. To pray we simply need to open our mouths and begin a conversation.

A spoken prayer is the fastest-working therapy in the world because it is the most natural. It reveals every man at his truest and best, because in real prayer every man checks in at zero on the register. He comes not trusting in himself but asking for help. I have never known a stammerer to stammer when he was talking intimately to God. In counseling with people I usually endeavor to get them to pray aloud: nothing else tells me so clearly whether their problems have a solution.

Recently I talked with a lady whose hair had turned white at forty, who had stopped working and was fearful that she was losing her mind. There were some superficial signs of neurosis, but when she prayed with me her prayer was utterly lucid and rational, and pointed in the direction she wanted to go—to wholeness. It did not take much insight to conclude that she was spiritually sound. Within a few weeks she had talked and prayed her way through her fear symptoms and had gone back to work.

Many people object to verbalized prayer because it makes them feel self-conscious, as if there were really "nothing there" and they were talking to themselves like mutterers on the street. The truth is that in prayer it is impossible to talk to oneself. Frank Laubach tells of a young man who remarked to him archly that prayer

8

was nothing more than mere autosuggestion. Dr. Laubach replied, "My boy, God can use autosuggestion." A West Coast minister, Robert Boyd Munger, has challenged anyone to pray fervently to Jesus Christ for five consecutive minutes—aloud—without finding his life dynamically redirected.

Our prayers start where we are, in poverty of spirit. If we continue to wait and our prayers seem to others to grow richer in spirituality, it can only mean one thing: that we are really becoming poorer in spirit as God proceeds with His pruning and stripping. The way of the Cross is the way to God, but it is not a way up, it is a way down.

The men of the Bible were keenly aware of their spiritual meanness. Their prayers are characterized not by demands but by self-emptyings. Listen to this prayer of Hezekiah the king in the days of Isaiah: "I said, I shall not see the Lord, even the Lord, in the land of the living. . . . Like a crane or a swallow, so did I chatter: I did mourn as a dove: mine eyes fail with looking upward: O Lord, I am oppressed; undertake for me." (Isaiah 38:11, 14)

Out of his desperation Hezekiah received an answer, and his rejoicing is still contagious after twenty-seven centuries: "What shall I say? he hath both spoken unto me, and himself hath done it. . . . O Lord, by these things men live. . . . The living, the living, he shall praise thee, as I do this day. . . ." (Isaiah 38:15–16, 19)

The prayers of the early apostles had the same characteristic note. "We know not what we should pray for as we ought," says Paul, "but the Spirit [himself] maketh intercession for us with groanings which cannot be uttered." (Romans 8:26) Instead of being "mighty men of prayer," the apostles were "unmighty men of not-prayer," yet God gave them both prayer and power in the midst of their poverty.

4

There is a sense in which we can find the whole Bible a commentary on this Beatitude. From peak to peak, from Mount Moriah where Abraham prepared to sacrifice Isaac, to Mount Calvary where Jesus of Nazareth endured the humiliation of a Roman gallows, the cry is echoed: "The poor in spirit shall enter the kingdom!"

Abraham went to God with absolutely nothing; he walked out of his father's house "not knowing whither," not even knowing who had called him. Thus was he rendered fit for the Lord's summons.

Moses was probably the most unpromising prospect for leadership that a people ever had, yet he goes down in history as one of the greatest. He had an Egyptian name, a speech impediment, a weak set of knees, an ugly disposition, a criminal record, and a price on his head; he was despised by Hebrew and Egyptian alike. His life was bankrupt, and because of that, God could use him.

I am fond of the story of David in the cave of Adullam. It is a perfect illustration of what Jesus was talking about. David was being hunted down like an animal by the king's troopers. He was hiding in the meanest hole in a primitive and poverty-stricken land, and his crew matched the environment. "Everyone that was in distress, and everyone that was in debt, and everyone that was discontented, gathered themselves unto him; and he became a captain over them." (I Samuel 22:2) They had nothing to lose, and were ready for anything—even for God. That meant God could do something with them, and He did. He met David with blessing upon blessing, even to the royal scepter. The dispirited became the vehicle of the Holy Spirit.

There are other fascinating illustrations of the Beatitude in Scripture. The widow of Zarephath welcomed Elijah into her home when the household was on the verge of starvation. "I have not a cake," she said, "but an handful of meal in a barrel, and a little oil in a cruse: and . . . I am gathering two sticks, that I may go in and dress it for me and my son, that we may eat it, and die." (I Kings 17:12) The prophet Elijah might have been discouraged by this lack of provender, since the Lord had told him that the widow would "sustain" him. Instead, Elijah found that it was the *lack* that set up conditions so that God could act. He told her to prepare what she had, and the Lord would take care of the rest—which He did. The cruse of oil became a cup running over, a symbol of divine blessing. Centuries later Jesus Christ added a footnote to this story. He pointed out that the woman of Zarephath was not even one of "God's people," as the Israelites called themselves.

Mary, the mother of Jesus, seems to have been a wisp of a Galilean peasant girl about whom very little is known. If she had noble character and distinguished ancestry, she did not trade on it. She speaks of herself as the "hand-maiden of the Lord" of "low degree" and "low estate." Luther suggests that if God had wanted human nobility and honor for His Son, He could have chosen Caiaphas' daughter to bear Him. Instead, God found that Mary's qualities—or lack of qualities—were eminently usable. Experts may differ on how Mary might have scored in a modern intelligence or personality test, but this is sure: in the test of spirit the Lord seeks out the low score, and Mary qualified.

Jesus in effect illustrates the Beatitude in parable after parable: the beggars are called in and banqueted after the guests fail to make their appearance; the young prodigal sinks to the status of the swineherd and even of the swine. When he has nothing, he remembers his father's house. The story of the rich young ruler makes us see that it is not enough even to know the commandments and the catechism. The young man turns away from Jesus sorrowfully, for without a broken spirit he cannot follow.

The most remarkable thing about Pentecost was not that the early apostles were all "of one accord" or that they spoke in many languages. The most remarkable thing was their poverty of spirit—they were empty, so they could be filled.

The Apostle Paul drives home the point in a hundred ways. He tells how the Savior of men "made himself of no reputation" for our sakes. How those words cut across our pride! Think of the infinite pains we take to erect our own reputations. Our character is our masterpiece, representing a lifetime effort to lay claim to honor among men. Yet Jesus (as Paul says) took the form of a slave, and humbled Himself, and became obedient unto death. (Philippians 2:7-8) As for Paul, there are many who consider him the second greatest man who ever lived. Certainly he traveled to spiritual high places that leave the rest of us earthbound. Yet near the close of his life he wrote a very simple epitaph for himself. It was: "The Chief of Sinners."

5

Goodspeed translates this Beatitude, "Blessed are they who feel their spiritual need." There is not one of us who will not face at some time the gap between what he is and what he ought to be as a Christian. It is good to learn at the beginning, therefore, to accept ourselves not as we ought to be but as we really are, because at the Cross we find God accepting us in our misery and poverty. We are prepared for the "exchanged life" that Hudson Taylor speaks of, as God takes away even our rags that He might clothe us in the glorious raiment of His righteousness.

In answer to our prayer the message of this Beatitude comes as a gift of hope: our heavenly Father takes us as we are, with all of our lack and shortcoming. The only requirement He makes is that we come with an empty vessel. And here is the promise: that men's extremity is God's opportunity, and that our place of despair shall become the scene of Christ's atoning victory.

Thomas Hooker was a beloved Puritan preacher who

is honored in New England today as the father of constitutional liberty. As he lay dying in Hartford, the members of his flock gathered around him and sought to comfort him. "Brother Thomas," they said, "yours has been a life of great achievement and piety; now you go to claim your reward." Hooker retorted, "I go to claim mercy."

No pretense, no contrived "front" will do before God, who treats all "fronts" as whited sepulchers, and checks every man's luggage before the final journey. Thus the paradox: the spiritually rich are the spiritually empty. How easy it is to say, and how difficult to learn! So much in modern life seems to teach the exact opposite.

For example, in suburban America today there is a strong drift to the churches on the part of young married couples. Are they being drawn by a deep hunger, a sense of spiritual need or a conviction of their sinful state? A revealing survey was made by William H. Whyte, Jr., in this connection.[1] In one suburban community Mr. Whyte found that the residents considered their churches to be "prestige groups" where social values were to be gained by being included. Salvation seems to have been the last thing in anyone's mind. People joined the house of God for friendship, stability, and "belongingness." What factors made them choose one church rather than another? Here they are in order of importance: *first*, the minister; *second*, the Sunday school; *third*, the location; *fourth*, the denomination; and *fifth*, the music. Somewhere in the mechanics of motivation the Gospel was overlooked.

[1] *The Organization Man*, Doubleday & Co., Inc., New York, 1957.

Mr. Whyte does not comment on the results of his door-to-door findings. He does not have to. His statistics reveal all too clearly that there is an "infinite qualitative difference" between signing the roll of a local church and entering into the Kingdom of Heaven. Yet Jesus Christ exacts the same requirements in suburbia that he does anywhere: poverty of spirit. The survey only highlights the Beatitude. Christ died for those in the tracts as He died for those across the tracks. All are leveled at the Cross and there is no difference. The only kind of prestige that counts with God is that which is sealed by the blood of His Son. The only social value He honors is our love for each other, which is His love shining through.

Here then is our Lord's meaning: the spiritually rich are the spiritually empty. "That which thou sowest is not quickened, except it die." (I Corinthians 15:36) But when God finds that at last the road has been cleared of debris and obstruction, He comes in with power.

So we see that our pilgrimage will be a different kind of journey from any we have ever taken. In science and in education we proceed with experimental faith from the known to the unknown, but to walk into the land of blessing we must forget even what we "know." Only in the spiritual world must the Pharisee leave his post of attainment, beat his breast alongside the publican, and declare that he possesses nothing of his own. Only in personal encounter with Jesus Christ do we surrender everything and declare our way to have been the way of failure, that it may become the way to the Cross.

It is when we let go of the rope that we discover that underneath are the everlasting arms. It is when we have no spirit at all that we receive the gift of the Holy Spirit. "We have this treasure in earthen vessels, that the excellency of the power may be of God, and not of us." (II Corinthians 4:7)

BLESSED ARE THEY THAT MOURN:

FOR THEY SHALL BE COMFORTED.

2

Beauty for Ashes

I

THE BEATITUDE is saying quite simply that if we mourn, we shall receive comfort and blessing, and that if we do not, the blessing will be withheld. It thereby faces us with a dilemma, for to many of us mourning is a lost art. We scarcely know what it means, and how can we practice it? The word has slipped out of our vocabulary.

Until quite recent times mourning was a well-recognized human activity. Even in our own country special clothing was prescribed for the mourners: the arm bands, the widow's weeds, the mourning cloak. Not only was there mourning for death, there was mourning for sin. In many churches of a hundred years ago the front pew was reserved as a "mourner's bench" for worshipers who were under conviction by the Holy Spirit.

Today it is a mark of the age that we do none of these things. If we do not whistle in public, neither do we mourn. We simply try to carry on and battle it through. We may be upset, we may analyze our case histories, we may fall apart, we may leap from a bridge, but we do not mourn.

It becomes important to discover what Jesus means by this Beatitude. *Why should we mourn?*

Let us start at the Cross. Perhaps the view from Calvary will give us the right perspective. Who were the mourners at the Cross? There were Mary the mother of Jesus, Mary Magdalene, and Mary the wife of Cleophas, and perhaps Salome. A few men mourned, too, scattered through the jeering and whipped-up crowd. There were Joseph of Arimathaea, and Nicodemus, and John, and the Roman centurion, and one of the thieves. Not many, considering the size of the throng. Was there another? Yes, one more: Jesus Christ Himself. As He hung on the Cross, He mourned, and we would do well to study His grief first.

Jesus Christ mourned with compassion for His fellow man: "Father, forgive them; for they know not what they do." His sensitivity embraced everything from the fall of the sparrow to an obscure widow's eviction. He mourned first of all for the human race that ignored the free gift of life He offered, and that felt it "expedient" (to use the word of Caiaphas) to crucify Him. He pitied the thralldom of disease and sin and death in which His brethren were held. We cannot understand the radiance of Jesus' life until we understand that He was one who

18

mourned—at the grave of Lazarus, on the brow of Jerusalem, in Gethsemane and on the Cross.

If we seek the kinetic power of the Christian life, therefore, we have uncovered a secret clue; it is mourning. Some call it "concern." Some call it "carrying a burden." Others, "being sensitive to human need." Take this quality out of human life and you have destroyed humanity. Develop it and the race is blessed.

Compassionate mourning can take a variety of forms. A mother's heart skips a beat when she hears of the suffering of a child: this is mourning. An honest citizen is shocked to learn of the bad news that has come to a neighbor: this is mourning. God uses such hearts creatively, and gives them strength and *comfort*. The pitiable person is not the mourner but the one who finds his solace in other people's woes. For him God provides no blessing; instead there is the ominous suggestion of the word of the Lord to Malachi: "I will curse your blessings."

Spiritual awakening has never come to a people who have not mourned. No one can become a truly evangelical Christian without having been given a burden for the salvation of his fellow man. Paul declared, "I say the truth in Christ . . . that I have great heaviness and continual sorrow in my heart. For I could wish that myself were accursed from Christ for my brethren . . . that they might be saved." (Romans 9:1–3; 10:1) It was out of such a concern that the Christian faith sprang, and when that concern dies, Christianity will die. We need to remind ourselves of this truth. No sociological goals, no "adapted programs for special community needs" will compensate for the drive to seek out the lost. The Gospel goes where the mourners go.

2

We are to mourn not only for the suffering of the world, but for the sin of the world, including our own sin. Walt Whitman wrote some well-known lines in *Leaves of Grass* which expressed his admiration for "the animals" who are "so placid and self-contained" and "do not lie awake in the dark and weep for their sins." The verse was intended not as a compliment to animals but as a rebuke to Christians of a certain type. Unfortunately, it threw the whole moral question into the animal kingdom. The capacity to be sorry for one's sins is one of the distinguishing marks of true humanity, that is to say, of humanity under God. The sensitive conscience may be the butt of much of the world's spite, but it is God's strongest weapon in the soul of man.

When Peter pleaded, "Depart from me; for I am a sinful man, O Lord!" (Luke 5:8), he was going through the same ordeal of fire that every Christian must undertake within himself. The life in Christ is not a life of constant introspection but it does require periodic self-examination. If our prayers are all praise and thanksgiving or all supplication and intercession, without any attention to the shortcomings and failures of our daily walk, it is not long before our lives begin to show serious deformity. The psychologists who would rid their patients of all guilt feelings are as wrong as the preachers of law without Grace. How can anyone ever absorb the New

Testament teaching of forgiveness through the Lord Jesus Christ until he has come to a state of mourning for his sins? Jesus is no Savior until we are aware of our need to be saved.

The Israelite mourned not only for his own sins but for those of his nation. Do you remember the cry of Isaiah before God in the temple? "Woe is me! for I am undone; because I am a man of unclean lips, and I dwell in the midst of a people of unclean lips. . . ." (Isaiah 6:5) At the Wailing Wall of Jerusalem the succeeding generations for well over two thousand years have mourned, not just for the misfortune of the Babylonian exile, but for the national sin that, according to their prophets, was rewarded by God's judgment in the exile. By the same token, the healthiest thing that could happen to America today would be a period of nation-wide mourning. For what? For events of the past, or the present, or for dread of the future? No; rather for the *sin* that brings judgment upon a people.

When a Christian thinks of such incidents as have taken place at Little Rock and Birmingham, he may feel an impulse to take remedial action: to write a letter, to join a group, to make a contribution, or to treat his fellow man with more love. Such impulses are right and good. What happened at Little Rock and Birmingham, however, requires of God's people more than social activity; it calls for *mourning*. Without that grief and sorrow, well-intended social action so often turns out to be mostly nervous reaction. It takes tears to make an ethical action real, otherwise it is simply indignation—it is

Peter cutting off the ear of Malchus. Blessed are they that mourn, for *they* shall be comforted.

Moon races and arms races continue to soak up our brainpower. Can anyone contemplating the "scientific advance" since Hiroshima doubt that somewhere, somehow, the human race has acquired a fatal defect or flaw that is really a passport to doom? The old Dutch doctor in one of Somerset Maugham's South Seas yarns remarked, "Life is short, nature is hostile and man is ridiculous." When we think of the infinite possibilities for good that lie within the human breast, of the tremendous resourcefulness of men, their courage and sacrifice in adversity, their capacity for love and kindliness, and then see what the race is up to, what can we Christians do but mourn?

Consider Jesus of Nazareth, the most generous-hearted person who ever lived. He never refused a request for help. "Great multitudes followed him, and he healed them all." (Matthew 12:15) He went out of His way to cross racial and religious barriers. He compassed the whole world in His love. Study Him as He set His face to go to Jerusalem: note the honest way in which He dealt with friends and opposition alike; see how each interview left Him stronger in reliance upon His Father and nobler in the eyes of men. In the midst of the tension and controversy that surrounded Him there was a calm that can only be described as holy. It was a good life, a glorious life, and it ended with all the vulgarity of a street accident.

God pity us if we do not mourn for the tragedy of

22

life as it is lived out, and has been lived since our first parents, in sin compounded and woe multiplied. Yet the Gospel proclaims that in the midst of such mourning—not in spite of it, and not to the left or right of it—we are blessed.

3

A natural cause of mourning is the transitoriness of life. Death is the raw material of the poets, who have turned mourning into a fine art. Thus Shakespeare:

> Out, out, brief candle,
> Life's but a walking shadow

and Keats:

> She dwells with Beauty—Beauty that must die

and Shelley:

> O weep for Adonais, he is dead

and Tennyson:

> Thou madest man, he knows not why,
> He thinks he was not made to die;
> And thou hast made him: thou art just.

and Arnold:

> And we are here as on a darkling plain

and Fitzgerald:

> A Moment's Halt—a momentary taste
> Of Being from the Well amid the Waste—

23

And, Lo! the phantom Caravan has reach'd
The Nothing it set out from

and Thompson:

Whether man's heart or life it be which yields
Thee harvest, must Thy harvest-field
Be dunged with rotten death?

Noble as are these expressions of pathos, they cannot match the description of death in the words of Scripture:

Because man goeth to his long home,
and the mourners go about the streets:
    or ever the silver cord be loosed,
    or the golden bowl be broken,
    or the pitcher be broken at the fountain
    or the wheel broken at the cistern.

(Ecclesiastes 12:5–6)

The Christian Gospel has never dodged the truth: earth to earth, ashes to ashes, dust to dust. Yet there are those who consider it indecent to mourn for death; who believe that tears in a Christian suggest a lack of equipoise. Mourning is even classified by some shallow interpreters of modern living with melancholia and manic depression. Better psychologists, however, know that the mourners have always been a healthier people than those of a more stoical frame of mind. The rigid shutting off of bodily juices in the face of tragedy so often manages to turn people into something less than men. The discipline that masks all feeling in a show of bravado or *sangfroid* is a fool's discipline. It plays ostrich with reality, for the truth is that every human being is doomed. The mark of fate is upon each of us; we may eat, drink, and be merry, but tomorrow *we die*. It is the mourner who comes to grips with this reality; so that, far from being a victim of gloom, he is made through Christ the conqueror of it.

To illustrate, a father who suffers the bereavement of a beloved child may go through his personal catastrophe dry-eyed. He may consider any betrayal of emotion to be a sign of weakness or even of lack of faith. He may sternly "carry on" his daily life without interruption. In such an experience even though we may not mourn outwardly, our bodies do. In odd, strange ways, not always healthy, the heart serves notice that it is dressed in black; for man is mortal, and he cannot help mourning his mortality. How much better that grief should express itself in normal fashion; how much more comfort in true mourning!

The Scriptures suggest a link between human nature (the problem of sin) and human destiny (the certainty of death). "By one man sin entered into the world, and death by sin; and so death passed upon all men, for that all have sinned." (Romans 5:12) Without going into all the implications of the passage, we can see that Paul is suggesting that the shortness of life is bound up with the evil in the world. When Mary Magdalene stood weeping at the tomb of Jesus, her heart was broken not only because of the Life that had been extinguished, but because of the deed that caused it. To mourn for sin and to mourn for death are but two sides of the same cloth. The poets have always known it. It is important for us to learn it too.

4

Note the absoluteness of the Beatitude's statement: the blessing will not fail to come. Comfort, of course, is derived from the words "con" and "fort" meaning "with strength," and behind the promise of this word stands the resurrection of Jesus Christ, where total defeat was turned into glorious victory. Thus the valley of the shadow of death becomes our main highway to the life of goodness and mercy. There are no side exits; it is a throughway, a turnpike. If we mourn, things will be better. God will bless.

There is a passage in Isaiah which follows immediately after the famous verses quoted by Jesus Christ in the synagogue at Nazareth. (Luke 4:18) The passage reads:

> The spirit of the Lord God is upon me . . . to comfort all that mourn . . . to give unto them beauty for ashes, the oil of joy for mourning, the garment of praise for the spirit of heaviness; that they might be called trees of righteousness, the planting of the Lord, that he might be glorified. (Isaiah 61:1, 2, 3)

There are no more beautiful phrases in the English language, but there is more here than literary excellence.

The promise to the Christian is that "if we be dead with him, we shall also live with him: if we suffer, we shall also reign with him." (II Timothy 2:11, 12) The distinction between worry and mourning is that one brings enslavement, the other, release.

If we possess that sensitivity of spirit that enables us to enter into the agony of mankind, we shall be given in reward the lifting of the Spirit who will keep us from being smothered by the agony. If we make our "quiet time" of worship a period of genuine empathy, of sorrow in prayer, of participation and involvement in what may well seem (humanly speaking) to be the death throes of the race, then there is hope for us. If God will not honor our service, He may honor our tears.

Peter taught us that the sufferings of Jesus Christ are a pattern for us to follow. John painted on a mighty canvas the picture of those who "came out of great tribulation, and have washed their robes, and made them white in the blood of the Lamb." (Revelation 7:14) Paul and Silas received the garment of praise for the spirit of heaviness, as, with sore backs, they sang songs at midnight in the jail at Philippi.

> Some through the water,
>   Some through the flood,
> Some through the fire,
>   But all through the blood;
> Some through great sorrow,
>   But God gives a song
> In the night seasons
> And all the day long.

The comfort of this Beatitude means, finally and precisely, joy: beauty for ashes, and the oil of joy for mourning. But joy is not simply a sentimental word like pleasure or happiness. Joy has a clean tang and bite to it, the exhilaration of mountain air. Joy, according to the Letter to the Hebrews, is what sent Jesus of Nazareth to the Cross. It was a joy in prospect, and for the Christian, fulfillment today is never complete; there is always joy in prospect. That final joy is suggested in John Bunyan's description of the death of Valiant for Truth in *Pilgrim's Progress:* "So he passed over and all the trumpets sounded for him on the other side." That is how a Christian goes home!

Meanwhile there is a gladness that is real and that is present. The disciples felt it when, in the days following the Crucifixion, Jesus appeared and stood in their midst (John 20:20). He bore "tidings of comfort and joy," for no one can mourn or weep for long when Jesus is around. The things He brings are cheer and courage and good news. Depressed spirits simply cannot stay depressed in His presence.

Today in the name of Jesus great world-wide organizations are engaged in a ceaseless task of providing comfort for the mourners: One Great Hour of Sharing, The Salvation Army, Church World Service, the Red Cross, World Vision, and others. As they feed the hungry and clothe the naked and provide shelter for the homeless, they are bringing the same good cheer that Christ spread wherever He went. Even more, the Church that unashamedly proclaims the New Testament message of salvation is bringing comfort that is genuine rejoicing, for it is producing God's richest fruit in new men and women.

All this was made possible through the Cross. Jesus spoke repeatedly of the meaning of His forthcoming suffering, death, and resurrection, yet none of the disciples understood. Had they done so, they would not have been scattered and confused at the last. They did not see what the Savior saw, that while man crucified Him intentionally and "meant it to him for evil," God meant it to Him for good. If there had been no ashes of Gehenna there would have been no beauty of the Resurrection. If there had been no atoning death there would have been no redemption. No mourning, no joy—and no blessing.

We can be glad that God raised up mourners, for to them He gave comfort that leaps beyond the Cross, beyond the Resurrection, even beyond Pentecost, and takes us into the very heart of the Book of Acts and the glorious, joyful life of the early Church.

5

As we distinguish the true meaning of "mourning" we find it necessary to sift out the false. Mourning, as Jesus described it, must never be construed to suggest self-pity. Preoccupation with one's own woes, carping, and plaintiveness have no stake in this Beatitude. Jesus certainly did not teach, "Blessed are they that moan"!

A letter was shown me from one who has steadfastly refused to be reconciled to the death of a mate. "After all these years I still cannot accept it," the letter ran, "I just grieve—and grieve—and grieve."

All of us recognize that there is a kind of mourning that is a drag upon life. It is perhaps better described not as mourning but as mournfulness. Some mournful types tend to give healthy-minded Christians the "creeps." They seem to cast such a pall over everything, and to try to turn existence into an endless dirge. Nothing is ever right. Even the topic of the weather becomes a conversational maneuver to expose one's miseries in a fresh appeal for sympathy. The chirping of the "Pity-Me Bird" can be insatiable as well as incessant.

We have seen that mourning, as we have considered it, exemplifies the Spirit and mind of Christ, but the mournfulness of which I now speak more closely resembles the Pharisee. The former suggests the divine compassion of our Lord, the latter indicates a psychological state of depression. The one offers relief and release through divine blessing, the other offers a prospect of solid and perpetual gloom.

"Moaning," if I may use the expression, is nevertheless one of the favorite activities of the human race. Psychiatrists are paid as high as fifty dollars an hour to listen to it. Divorce complaints in county courthouse files are filled with it. Everybody does it; sometimes it seems that to meet is to talk is to "moan." Yet nowhere in Scripture is it promised that the "moaners" will be comforted or blessed, and life upholds the Word of God. It is the bitter lesson of experience that the man who builds Dismal Castle will have to live in it. Those who make the most of trifles will eventually be given a condition worthy of their exercises in complaining.

My wish for you is that by the Grace of God you may become a true mourner; that by His Spirit you may be empowered to put aside the daily ration of gripe and beef, and capture again the vision of your vocation as a son or daughter of God. How much more easily we run the race of life, when these weights are dropped off! Then we learn anew the rich, strong meaning of "comfort": not comfort that lulls or coddles like a hot-water bottle or a baby's pacifier; but comfort "with strength" that sounds a trumpet note of deliverance! "Speak ye comfortably to Jerusalem, and cry unto her, that her warfare is accomplished." (Isaiah 40:2)

We take our leave of this Beatitude with thanksgiving and with a promise to return to it, for we have learned much. We have discovered—what we already suspected —that the growth and maturity of a Christian is not achieved simply by leaping from one joyous experience to another. There is a process of mourning that must also be passed through; and it could well be said that man is most truly man when he mourns, for out of the crucible God molds the polished instrument, fit for the hand of the Master. Out of the spirit of heaviness the new man emerges, clad in the garment of praise. So long as his mourning is according to the mind of Christ, the Christian is secure in the knowledge of blessing.

BLESSED ARE THE MEEK:

FOR THEY SHALL INHERIT THE EARTH.

3

When the Last Are First

I

AS WE MOVE further into our study we are discovering the need for inward discipline. The Beatitudes, we find, are really "hard sayings"; they are flexing muscles that we have not used for a long time, and we are not sure whether the struggle is worth it. Especially do we feel discouraged when we come to the third Beatitude, for while the words say, "Blessed are the meek," we are semantically conditioned to think, "Blessed are the weak." The Sunday school hymn couplet went, "Gentle Jesus meek and mild, look upon this little child," and so we say that we know what meekness is: it is weakness, softness, gentleness, docility; to be meek is to be something less than a man, it is to be tame, passive, yielding. It is to be womanly, as woman is of the weaker sex.

Does not the "meek little man" bring up immediately

32

the spineless image of Casper Milquetoast? Does not the "meek little wife" turn out to be the one who lets her husband "get away with murder"?

We could not be more wrong. The meek are not weak: they are so strong, says Jesus, that they shall inherit the earth. They are mightier than any breed the human race has produced from blood and soil. They control more power than is found in interplanetary space, for they have access to the Creator. Their battle cry is the song of Deborah against the Canaanite host under Sisera (Judges 5:20, 31): "They fought from heaven; the stars in their courses fought against Sisera . . . So let all thine enemies perish, O Lord." The men who have written history's most impressive pages have been meek men, and when the latest tyranny to afflict the earth's surface is removed, it will be meek men who will do it.

Who are these men? What is the trait that Jesus Christ is describing in them? How can we gain it for ourselves?

Let us move out into full view of the Cross and begin from there. Calvary presents a grim historical picture of an itinerant carpenter and teacher being executed on trumped-up charges of sedition and heresy. To the eye of faith, however, there is evident also the deliberate self-sacrifice of God's only-begotten Son, who was seeking to obey His Father's will. The Gospels teach that He laid down His life not because He was trapped by a false apostle or lynched by wicked men, but because He wished to fulfill the Scriptures by atoning for the sin of

33

the world. "I have a baptism to be baptized with; and how am I straitened till it be accomplished!" (Luke 12:50) It was His own decision, arrived at only after much agony of Spirit; He literally "learned obedience by the things that He suffered." He obeyed, He underwent the discipline, and He finished the work, and throughout He exhibited—meekness.

Thus the meek man is not necessarily a passive personality at all. The meek of whom Jesus speaks are those who have chosen to heed the voice of God and to place themselves in the center of His will. They have followed their Savior to the Cross and have put their lives upon the block. In their obedience they have shown the *capacity to take it*. Meekness, says Archbishop Trench, is "an inwrought grace of the soul, and the exercises of it are first and chiefly towards God." At the Cross we see the God-centered quality of meekness. Jesus Christ, who seized the initiative from Herod, from Pilate and even from John the Baptist, now obeys His Father's will to the yielding up of His life.

The Cross teaches us a definition of meekness that will keep us from ever being bothered by this word again: *we must be nothing, that God might be everything*. Thus the meek are not simply the jaunty, as some would attempt to derive from the French translation of our Beatitude: "*Heureux les débonnaires; car ils hériteront de la terre*." Nor are they those who possess a vague "faith in the friendliness of the universe" (Ligon). First and foremost, the blessed meek are those who have given over their lives to the Savior that He might live in them.

34

Does the Bible confirm the view of meekness we see from the Cross?

It is a fairly simple process to take the original tongues of Scripture and to read back into the Hebrew and Greek an interpretation of a word or phrase that fits our presuppositions, not to say our prejudices. It is not so easy to approach the Bible objectively and *meekly*, and to ask what it is seeking to teach us. In fact, one of the real hurdles for the modern Christian is the Bible itself.

Many of us are modest enough in our daily walk, but our attitude toward the written sources of the Christian faith can become quite patronizing. The men who wrote the Bible were not moderns, we say, they were ancients; and how can they teach us? Our intellectual *hauteur* exudes when we acquire a little background of Bible history. We approach the sacred page with condescension; whatever the problem the text poses, we can "explain" it. How sharply the scalpel of this Beatitude severs the root of our criticism, for it tells us that our pride has neutralized its own argument! Only the scientist who sits down before the facts as a little child learns the secrets of nature; and only the meek have an inheritance in Scripture. "Receive with meekness the engrafted word, which is able to save your souls," advises James. Received any other way, the salt has lost its savor; the Bible is stripped of its life-giving power.

By comparing Scripture with Scripture we make

remarkable discoveries about this Beatitude. Like several others its roots are found in the Psalms. The very wording of the 37th Psalm is significant:

> Those that wait upon the Lord, they shall inherit the earth. For yet a little while, and the wicked shall not be: yea, thou shalt diligently consider his place, and it shall not be. But the meek shall inherit the earth.
>
> (Psalm 37:9-11)

Further in the Psalms we read:

> The meek shall eat and be satisfied. (Psalm 22:26)
>
> The meek will he guide in judgment: and the meek will he teach his way. (Psalm 25:9)
>
> The Lord lifteth up the meek. (Psalm 147:6)
>
> Let them praise his name in the dance: let them sing praises . . . with the timbrel and harp. For the Lord taketh pleasure in his people: he will beautify the meek with salvation. (Psalm 149:3-4)

Aaron and Miriam challenged Moses' authority by asking, "Hath the Lord indeed spoken only by Moses? hath he not spoken also by us?" (Numbers 12:2) The text then relates that "Moses was very meek, above all the men which were upon the face of the earth." There is no suggestion that Moses was subservient to his brother or sister; his attitude was rather one of forbearance, while his humility was directed toward God. To see Moses meek, see him standing barefoot and wordless before the Lord on the rocks of Sinai.

When the churches of Galatia are instructed by

Paul (Galatians 6:1) how to administer church discipline to a brother found in error, they are warned, "Restore such a one in the spirit of meekness." Again, Peter tells the Christians of Asia (1 Peter 3:15) to be "ready always to give an answer to every man that asketh you a reason of the hope that is in you with meekness and fear." Both verses suggest that the man of meekness is under divine authority. He is humble because he realizes that his own spiritual standing lies in the Grace of God and not in any achievement of his own. He is meek because he is submitting to the discipline of the hand of God the Father. Jesus Christ Himself submitted to that discipline, and left the pattern.

Perhaps one of the clearest illustrations we can find in Scripture is in Ezekiel. The Hebrew prophet of the exile was given a vision of the holiness of God which he describes in these words: "I saw as it were the appearance of fire, and it had brightness round about. . . . This was the appearance of the likeness of the glory of the Lord. And when I saw it, I fell upon my face." Blessed are the meek! Ezekiel, prone, heard a voice of One that spoke: "And he said unto me, Son of man, stand upon thy feet, and I will speak unto thee. And the spirit entered into me when he spake unto me, and set me upon my feet, that I heard him." (Ezekiel 1:27, 28; 2:1–2) God did not leave Ezekiel prostrate on the ground, but raised him up that he might speak boldly to the house of Israel.

Clearly there are set forth in all these passages characteristics that we do not ordinarily associate with the concept of meekness. Even stronger than the promise of blessings to come is the note of discipline and teachableness. As Christ Himself expressed it, "Learn of me, for I am meek."

3

As a young university graduate I was eager to make a name for myself, to catch the eye of the nation in some sensational way. Depression days were propitious for dreaming, and out of my wool-gathering there emerged a new "beatitude": "Blessed are the colorful, for they shall make the world their oyster." Richard Halliburton, going round the world on a shoestring and writing his way to fame, seemed to hold the answer to life. I yearned to be a "creative personality" who would trip his way in sprightly fashion with a tip of the hat to anyone, even to God.

One stereotype perhaps above all others that I wished to avoid was the species known as "Jesus-lover" or—as we contemptuously referred to them—the "Christers." Their lives seemed to be dipped in pastel shades; their words sounded utterly dreary. What could be more undesirable than to surrender one's vitality and aggressiveness for a bland "goodiness," to immerse one's individuality in an ocean of piety? I would have laughed gaily at the fun that J. B. Phillips has since poked at a hymn which he says is "still sung in certain circles": [1]

[1] J. B. Phillips, *Your God Is Too Small*, The Epworth Press, London, 1952.

38

Oh to be nothing, nothing,
Only to lie at His feet,
A broken and emptied vessel
For the Master's use made meet.

Today I am not so willing to ridicule another man's faith. Today I am not so sure that the "colorful" are blessed, or that they are even colorful. When one has stood spiritually destitute alongside blind and ragged Bartimaeus, pleading with Jesus that he might receive his sight, and has felt the scales dropping from his eyes, he sees things differently. To my new eyes the creative personalities are those who radiate the love of their Lord. The Frank Laubachs, the Eugenia Prices, the Joy Ridderhofs, the Albert Schweitzers, the Billy Grahams, the "broken and emptied vessels" whom God has put together and used—in short, the meek: these are the ones who seem to hold the secret of life. The gallant Halliburton is lost on a daring but pointless adventure at sea, while the meek inherit the earth.

Who are the meek? If a man is willing to take Jesus Christ as his Savior and give up trying to save himself, he is meek. If he is willing to ascribe full glory to God and to give himself absolutely none, he is meek. If he is willing to desist trying to pit the spirit of man against the Spirit of God in contention, he is meek. God tells the meek man, "You shall be dead to every grade and rank among your fellow men. You shall seek the lowest place for yourself, and you shall seek it every day. You shall continue to dwell in it until you would not exchange it for a throne in heaven. You will rejoice every time that you are ignored and every time that your name is passed by."

If the man protests that this is a bit rough, God replies, "You will stay until it becomes smooth."

It makes no difference to the Lord whether a man be an extravert or an introvert; whether he be aggressive or retiring; whether his intelligence quotient be high or low. God the Creator is not looking for creative personalities at all, but for people that He can use, clay that He can mold, dust that He can breathe upon and cause to live.

4

To anyone who has read Thucydides, the present world struggle seems to be a replay of the Peloponnesian War. America, with her luxuriant culture and her traditions of freedom, wishing at all costs to preserve her way of life, is Athens *redivivus*. Soviet Russia is Sparta with her tight dictatorship, her allies among the have-not nations, and her total orientation toward combat. It was the fate of Athens to sink in the midst of her glory. The same fate, Toynbee reminds us, has overtaken scores of proud civilizations in the epic of man.

But if Athens was proud, certainly Sparta was not meek, and history records that the Spartan empire quickly fell apart. What the outcome of the present battle of titans will be, no one knows, but what we learn from the Greeks only reinforces the teaching of our Beatitude. The meekness that inherits the earth is compounded of more than discipline. It includes an element best described as the fear of the Lord. The Spartan knew nothing of this fear. His gods were made of plaster; he gave them the veneration of superstition. And when the clay gods fail to produce, as Pearl Buck shows us in *The Good Earth*, man turns on his idolatrous objects of worship and makes baseballs of them.

The fear of the Lord imparts a strange power to the believer. There is a suggestion of it in Julia Ward Howe's "Battle Hymn of the Republic." The Psalms are full of it. The character of Martin Luther was formed by it. It created Cromwell's "New Model Army," the best-behaved and most invincible force of men the world has ever known. The iron in the Puritan soul was tempered with it, and the Declaration of Independence was the result. In the Book of Proverbs we read that "the fear of the Lord is the beginning of wisdom." It could be said that this was the first statement of the theory of the survival of the fittest, for the God-fearing man is not easily intimidated by his fellows. It is also another way of saying that the meek shall inherit the earth.

Quite evidently we are discussing an element that is not too prominent in the twentieth century, and it is doubtful whether a crash program of nuclear construction in America is an adequate substitute. Unless the missile men and muscle men are also meek men, their labors are doomed: this is the plain teaching of the Word of God. In Charles Rann Kennedy's drama, *The Terrible Meek*,[2] the Roman centurion points out the flaw that eventually destroyed his empire:

[2] Harper & Brothers, New York, 1922.

41

"We go on building our kingdoms—the kingdoms of this world. We stretch out our hands, greedy, grasping, tyrannical, to possess the earth. Domination, power, glory, money, merchandise, luxury, these are the things we aim at; but what we really gain is pest and famine . . . dead and death-breathing ghosts that haunt our lives forever. . . . Possess the earth! We have lost it. We never did possess it. We have lost both earth and ourselves in trying to possess it."

Standing in the shadow of the Cross, the centurion utters the prophecy of the Beatitude:

"I tell you, woman, this dead son of yours, disfigured, shamed, spat upon, has built a kingdom this day that can never die. The living glory of Him rules it. The earth is *His* and He made it. . . . Something has happened up here on this hill today to shake all our kingdoms of blood and fear to the dust. . . . The meek, the terrible meek, the fierce agonizing meek, are about to enter into their inheritance."

The men of Sparta conquered and fell. They conquered because they were hardened warriors; they fell because they were not meek, and only the meek are blessed.

Our little systems have their day,
They have their day and cease to be.

Four centuries after Sparta there stood on Mars Hill in Athens a man named Paul who taught the worship of the one true God. Had the Athenians learned that lesson in Pericles' day, who knows what might have happened? The meek survive because they are fit to survive. Nothing can destroy them, neither angels nor principalities nor powers nor ICBMs nor cobalt bombs. They are invincible.

Meekness is like the surface of the water that is tossed by wind and storm, but when the tumult dies it invariably returns to its calm reflection of heaven. Meekness is a food soft to the palate, but it produces sinews of steel. Before God it bends to a humiliation beyond humility; before man it endures beyond endurance.

Were we to be sojourners in ancient Palestine and to discover Abraham, lying on his face before the altar of an unseen God, would we not question his balance and good judgment? Yet this same meek Abraham was given an inheritance like the sands of the seashore.

5

We learn from Jesus Christ that there is a meekness that we are to bear toward our brother, and even toward our enemy, and that it is subject to a daily conditioning by God Himself. It cannot be trusted to maintain its own level. When I attended the Chaplain School at Fort Devens during World War II, our instructor at the first session opened his Bible to Galatians 6:1 and read the words, "Brethren, if a man be overtaken in a fault, ye which are spiritual, restore such an one in the spirit of meekness; considering thyself, lest thou also be tempted." It does no good to prostrate ourselves before the Lord if we then proceed to be overbearing and arrogant toward our neighbor. The spirit of meekness is to be a continuing conditioner in teaching us to accept reproof and to face criticism objectively.

Perhaps the best way to relate the Beatitude to our daily lives is to consider driving in traffic. If there is one place where our century needs to understand the meaning of meekness, it is behind the wheel of an automobile. The qualities of patience, endurance, and courtesy make up the difference between life and death, and the Christian on the highway is God's man under discipline.

Remember that meekness does not mean servility and the meek man is not a door mat. Look again at the Gospel portrait of our Lord. Even in the washing of Peter's feet He maintained a dignity that transfigured the scene. There was a noble quality to His manliness that drew young and old. The compassion of His healing ministry flowed not from weakness but from strength. On the Cross where He took the worst that man could give Him, He held His head so high that even the admiration of a Roman legionary was kindled.

Meekness can best be contrasted with timidity as well as with aggressiveness by the figure of a door. Three men wish to go through the door; one is aggressive, one is timid, and one is meek. The aggressive man does not wait to see whether the door is locked, but hurls his weight against it and forces the latch. The timid man stands outside the door, dreading what is on the other side, afraid to try to enter. The meek man approaches the door and tests the knob to see whether the Lord has unlatched it. If He has, this man proceeds to walk in.

It is true in personal relationships and it is true of

our nation as a whole that we are short-rationed in this quality. God lets us toot our horns all we please, but He never blesses the result. What Jesus Christ is suggesting in this Beatitude is a measure long overdue: a revival of meekness. Today the world is weary of boasting; yet with the resurgence of nationalism there is little relief in prospect. How welcome would be a prophet who would speak for our time the words of Isaiah: "Produce your cause, saith the Lord; bring forth your strong reasons, saith the King of Jacob . . . yea, do good, or do evil, that we may be dismayed, and behold it together. Behold, ye are of nothing, and your work is of nought." (Isaiah 41:21, 23–24)

No one can lead another closer to Christ than he stands himself, and no nation can make another nation behave better than its own example. It is time to pray in our land for a spiritual awakening that will create a national meekness. We know that when it comes it will be of God and not of man. It will not be a contrived phenomenon. It may use the modern mass media and it may not. It may well take the form Shelton Smith suggested, of "a hard-bitten, psalm-singing band of religious revivalists." It may come through national suffering and disaster; certainly it cannot be expected to arrive on pillows of luxury. We can, if we will strip ourselves of some of the accoutrements of padded living, begin to prepare for the divine visitation.

In the book of Genesis we are told that God gave man "dominion . . . over all the earth." Man has not used that prerogative according to the rules; he has made his own rules, and the bully-boys have usurped the power wherever they could. Now we know that their day is doomed. The meek shall come into their own, not because they are deserving but because God has promised them a blessing. No gold stars are passed out in heaven for meekness, for it is by Grace we are saved. The Beatitude is, from beginning to end, simply an outpouring of divine Grace through Jesus Christ "so then it is not of him that willeth, nor of him that runneth, but of God that sheweth mercy." (Romans 9:16)

BLESSED ARE THEY WHICH DO HUNGER AND THIRST

AFTER RIGHTEOUSNESS: FOR THEY SHALL BE FILLED.

4

The Straight Line to God

I

HERE IS A STRANGE DECLARATION: so simple it is
passed over as obvious, so profound it is usually misun-
derstood. Were we to substitute the words, "Blessed are
they who keep struggling to do better; for they shall be
rewarded," we would express the meaning usually at-
tached to the Beatitude. We would then have a worthy
addition to the world's collection of platitudes and half
truths. We would also be doing a great injustice to the
words of Jesus. Our Beatitude says nothing about toil or
struggle. It says nothing about achievement or even
about improvement. Quite the contrary: it speaks of
men whose emptiness leaves them unable to work.

The deeper we get into our study, the more do the
Beatitudes stand out in bold relief, overarching the
maxims of men and the wisdom of this world. The

47

world cannot read the Sermon on the Mount; only the eye of faith is able to focus properly on the Word and to grasp what Jesus is teaching. The world reads the fourth Beatitude and thinks it is saying something about lifting ourselves by our bootstraps; faith senses that here is something closely akin to the cry from the Cross, torn out of the anguish of the soul of our Lord: "I thirst!"

It is common today for a community to honor one of its more active citizens by declaring him "Man of the Year." A profession or vocation finds it useful to select some prominent member and present him with an award. A philanthropist or a man of achievement will have a street, a park, a city or a mountain named after him. Of the honored one many will think, "He has arrived. His works of righteousness have been rewarded. He has reached the top. What more can he ask for, and what more can life provide?"

Yet the righteousness of which Christ speaks is not necessarily kind deeds or good citizenship. New Testament righteousness is not synonymous with goodness. Neither is righteousness to be confused with self-righteousness. Thus the upright man in the Bible is neither a do-gooder (in the tiresome sense) nor a prig.

The Old Testament concept of the seeker after righteousness is best symbolized by a pious Hebrew sitting under a fig tree, meditating on the law. The New Testament portrait is more dynamic. It conceives the seeker as possessed of a mission, a man stripped to essentials and basic drives: "this one thing I do." He is a man with desire, with hunger and thirst. His eye is "single."

48

His appetite will be appeased by no fleshly dainties. He is on a hunger strike for truth—about himself and his environment. Is he right with God or is he not; and, if he is not right, how can he be set right? Such a man, says Jesus Christ, will get his answer. He will get it not by dashing up and down mountains of moral effort, nor by aspiring after some distant Holy Grail of achievement, but by quietly starving out every other claim on himself.

That, perhaps, is why spirituality often has been associated with some kind of fasting. To miss a meal for God may not fill us with righteousness, but our relationship with Him is never quite the same afterward.

Right at the beginning, then, we must readjust our approach to the Beatitude. It seems so simple—if we go after a thing we will get it. "The Lord helps those who help themselves." Are we not so trained from childhood? Yet Jesus is not talking about a "thing," He is talking about righteousness. And in the Bible righteousness is always a condition before God rather than before men. Therefore, our Lord is speaking of what it takes for a man to be justified in God's sight, to be ripe for the Father's fellowship, so that he can walk and talk with his Lord freely and without rebuke. To do all this, says Jesus, takes more than man can muster. He must look for help beyond.

2

Two members of Grace Church met on a downtown street. Their thoughts naturally gravitated to their church and to the potluck supper scheduled for that evening. One asked, "What are you folks planning to bring?" The other replied, "My wife is away, so I'm bringing a good appetite!"

A poor enough way to conduct a potluck supper, you remark; but our subject is righteousness, and Jesus Christ says that the man's reply is exactly correct as far as righteousness with God is concerned. If he brings his hunger with him that is all he needs to bring; he will be filled. We are told that nature abhors a vacuum, but in the life of the Spirit it is different: God honors a vacuum and fills it to overflowing.

Before a man can be made righteous before God, then, he must be made "un-righteous." He must get rid of his "hot dishes and desserts"—the food of his own cooking. He must be relieved of the claptrap of the ego, the things that he considers commendable in his own eyes. It is a process so painful that Paul calls it crucifixion and Jesus Christ calls it something close to starvation. It is the spiritual leveling that takes place before the Cross.

The seeker finds that he has been hungering and thirsting after the wrong things, after forbidden fruit, and he has committed the sin of his first parents all over again. He discovers to his dismay that the sins on one side of Main Street are as offensive to God as the sins on the other side; "for there is no difference: For all have sinned, and come short of the glory of God." (Romans 3:22–23) He finds that the attitude that sustained him in life—perhaps best described as "I'm just as good as anybody else"—has actually distorted his vision and kept

50

him from facing reality. In short he finds a description of himself in Paul's words: "They being ignorant of God's righteousness, and going about to establish their own righteousness, have not submitted themselves unto the righteousness of God." (Romans 10:3)

Our Beatitude suggests that if a man yearns to be blessed with the righteousness of God he must first be stripped of the things that contaminate. In a defective environment, in a society that lives by compromise, we ask how such decontamination is possible. We know that the world steadfastly refuses to recognize that human nature can be changed. Do not the philosophers advise us that we are doomed to struggle through life half nobleman and half beast? In the words of James Branch Cabell, "Man plays the ape to his dreams."

When the cadres of Marxism announce dogmatically that in the future Communist society, when all "vestiges" of capitalism are removed, there will be no more thieving, molesting, or disturbing the peace, we laugh at their naïvete. We know better! Man does not educate himself out of his sins. And when we apply the same logic to the new birth we are tempted to pause in doubt. Are we really purified? Are we truly holy? Our friends ask us knowingly, is that halo dust on our shoulders or is it only dandruff? And then the final temptation of Satan: wouldn't it be better to relax in our dirt and contamination than to assume a virtue we do not possess?

The answer of the Gospel is like thunder from the seventh heaven: No! The God who made human nature can change human nature, and does! All efforts by the creature to make himself over are futile; "without me ye can do nothing." Our hope is in the Lord who saves and renews. We need not imagine that our fates are written in the stars; God made the stars too. By His Grace He has made a way for us out of the human predicament. That way is by the Cross, and it is by hunger and thirst. We must want God—want Him badly. "When thou saidst, Seek ye my face; my heart said unto thee, Thy face, Lord, will I seek." (Psalm 27:8)

We must want the righteousness of God so desperately that we are willing to label even our goodness as unfit for His holy sight. We simply cannot have it both ways: we cannot confess that we are sinners and at the same time seek to justify our acts. We cannot throw ourselves penitently on the mercy of the Lord and still try to preserve prestige and maintain our reputations. Christ did not die for noble beasts or beastly noblemen; He died for sinners, and He clothes only sinners who have discarded the rags of their own righteousness.

Thus the nails are slowly driven into our hands and feet, and the spear enters our side. We realize at last that we have reached the end of the road to Calvary. It is the moment of moments—the "existential" moment. For us all decks have been cleared, all planes have been grounded, all battlefields are quiet. There is darkness over the Place of the Skull, and silence in heaven for the space of half an hour. The clock at the heart of the universe seems to have run down. We know now what it means to be under the curse of sin. It is God's move.

3

God does not fail us. The moment we have divested ourselves of the rags we once thought becoming, the moment we reveal to Him our spiritual shame and nakedness, He hastens to us with cover. That is the great word of divine mercy in the Bible: *cover*. He covers our sins with His robe of righteousness.

At the age of seventeen I was inducted into a university fraternity by the process known as "hell week." After being exposed to the usual collegiate indignities for several hours I was flung into the fish pond and brought nude and shivering before the assembled chapter. My mortification was without limits; but at that point someone flung a quilt about my shoulders and covered me. I shall never cease to be grateful to that "brother"; the quilt's warmth and the kindness it symbolized after the ordeal fairly melted me, and the act is as vivid today as when it happened.

Since I have become a Christian I have been flung many times into a spiritual fish pond. The life of a believer was never calculated to inflate the ego—too much of the "id" is forever bubbling to the surface. And yet the promise of Scripture is unfailing: God covers our unrighteousness with His own righteousness.

How does He do it?

With the seamless robe of Jesus Christ.

When Christians speak of the "work" of Christ they do not refer to His woodwork in Joseph's carpenter

53

shop, or even to His labors of teaching and healing. They mean the work of establishing men before God, of making them worthy of the heavenly Father and holy and righteous in His eyes. Such is the work of the Cross.

The scene at Calvary cannot be made a pleasant one by any stretch of imagination or theology. The more we examine it the worse it becomes. What a ghastly business to have gone through! To study the Passion of our Lord is to realize that the real meaning of this Beatitude is: "Blessed are they that hunger and thirst after righteousness, for they shall be filled—*by me, through the Cross*." Seekers after righteousness do not find their reward automatically, as if life never fails, or as if the search itself is the reward. They are blessed because Christ atoned for them by interposing Himself in their stead.

If our sense of justice is annoyed by this, the annoyance is only a smoke screen to hide a greater issue. Far more deeply disturbing is the implication that each of us who believes owes more to Jesus Christ than to any person who ever lived. Not because He founded Western society, or gave to us the climate of democracy and science, or created the Church. Rather because He lifted the curse of unrighteousness from us and made us fit for the Kingdom of Heaven. "God commendeth his love toward us, in that, while we were yet sinners, Christ died for us." (Romans 5:8) And to break our cold and doubting hearts He did it gladly.

There is no greater work than Christ's—or harder work—and in a very real sense it is still being carried on. When I see the Lord at work on a human soul today

54

I stand back and gape in sheer admiration. I would never have dared to make the attempt. Even when Christ uses me to sow the seed, and I explain the Scriptures to an inquirer, a voice seems to whisper that my own personality defects are so glaring that the message will never come through. Thus when a proud, self-sufficient, ambitious soul comes crashing down at the base of the Cross I think, "Is it possible?" It is not easy to tell when a man is spiritually hungry or thirsty. "Spiritual things are spiritually discerned." I have been mistaken many times. Only the Holy Spirit is wise in these matters. He draws the heart in the first place. He riffles the water, kindles the fire, creates the appetite.

4

The deepest yearning in life is to know that our lives are somehow fulfilled and have meaning, that in spite of everything they "add up." Though we live in a tainted world that is forever rubbing off on us, we want the assurance that we pass muster, that we make the grade. We are eager to know that when the heavenly Father checks us over, instead of discarding us as "rejects," He will put on us His stamp of approval. We don't like to think that at the end of our span of years we are going to be picked up as "returned empties." We wish to be brought upstairs as "vessels of honor."

To know that he is right with God gives significance to every breath a Christian draws. Not to know it is to spend one's days seeking consolation in the markets and assemblies and revels of dissatisfied humanity. The world assures us that it is foolish to seek the righteousness of God, for it takes a genius to make a saint. Far better (argues the world) that we make an amiable adjustment to sin in this life, without, of course, overdoing it. The Scriptures reply that sainthood, like genius, is a gift, but a gift available to anyone. The robe of Christ fits everybody. The New Testament saints were not "canonized," they were simply people with faith. They did not earn their good standing with God, they received it from His hand as a gift, and only in that sense were they "gifted."

Anybody can find significance for his life in Jesus Christ. What Christ came to earth to do was not only to set men free but to set them right. His sacrifice was specifically to prepare us for fellowship with God here and hereafter. The heavenly Father welcomes us with open arms and imparts to us blessing upon blessing—not because we are upright but because Jesus Christ has clothed us with His own virtue.

There is a moving description in the Old Testament of Abraham pleading with God to spare the city of Sodom. Abraham asked first if God would destroy the city should there be fifty righteous men within it. The Lord replied that for the sake of the fifty righteous ones He would forego the destruction. Abraham then lowered the number to forty-five, then to forty, to thirty, to twenty, and finally to ten. The Lord replied each time, saying in turn that if such a number of righteous men were found in the city, He would spare the place. (Genesis 18:20–32)

Abraham stopped with ten, but no suggestion is given that the Lord's patience was exhausted. Had Abraham reduced the number to five, or three, or even to one righteous man, it cannot be inferred that he would have been refused a hearing. In fact, it is the teaching of the New Testament that for the sake of one righteous man the whole world has been offered a God-sent chance to avert its destruction and doom.

If we only knew it, Jesus Christ's righteousness is enough to cover all our lack of it. His love is enough to make up for our unloveliness. More than that, His Grace is able to take these virtues and to invest them in us, so that we become more like Him. When we hunger and thirst after Jesus, this Beatitude is fulfilled; for He is our righteousness. "If any man thirst, let him come unto me, and drink . . . from within him shall flow rivers of living water." (John 7:37, 38, ASV)

Jesus went to the Cross not only to bring us to God by conveying His righteousness to us, but also to show us what practical Christian living means today. As Chaucer wrote of his "poor parson":

> This noble ensample to his sheep he yaf,
> That first he wroghte, and afterward he taughte.

Jesus not only wrought upon the Cross, He also taught. He left us an example, and bade us take up our crosses and follow Him. He showed us how to quit ourselves like men, how to use the assurance of our righteous standing before God, not to lord it over our neighbors, but to help them. He showed us that true righteousness is nothing we can boast about, since it is only a borrowed cloak, dearly purchased, with ownership in heaven.

And it is the glory of the Gospel that for all the darkness of the road Christ leads us along, there is a light in the distance. Beyond Calvary shines the Resurrection. The way of the Cross is no nightmarish death march into oblivion, with just one sacrifice piled on another. It is a straight line to God. It leads home. The promise of this Beatitude is that in spite of everything that afflicts us on the way, in the end we shall be filled.

5

At one period in my life I carried on a running debate with myself on the question of questions: Why did Jesus Christ die for me?

He died for the world, perhaps; for the Church, to be sure; for "sin," so the apostle indicates; for the fulfillment of Old Testament prophecy, undoubtedly.

But for me?

I was being trained in a theological seminary with a deserved reputation for scholarship. I studied every "theory" of the atonement—penal, commercial, forensic, classical, moral influence, Anselmic. The strong and weak points of each were made known to me. I looked upon them with detached, twentieth-century objectivity. "Interesting historical phenomena," I thought, "but the mountain has labored and brought forth a mouse."

I learned that Jesus of Nazareth combined within Himself the concepts of the Son of Man as found in

Daniel, and the Suffering Servant as found in Isaiah; that the shedding of blood is necessary for the remission of sin because the cost of forgiveness is high; that a savior-figure is psychologically useful as a therapeutic agent to rid man of his guilt feelings.

None of these answers convinced me. None caused me to leap out of bed in the middle of the night, after the manner of Horace Bushnell, crying, "I have found it. I have found the Gospel!" They only left me more puzzled. Of all the reading of those years, I can remember only two passages that really spoke to my condition. One was a comment of Williston Walker, the church historian, in his discussion of theories of the atonement: "The message of the Gospel is that in some true sense Christ died, not for general justice, but for *me*." [1] The other was a passage in the journal of John Wesley, entered on Saturday, Feb. 7, 1736:

> Mr. Oglethorpe returned from Savannah with Mr. Spangenberg, one of the pastors of the Germans. I soon found what spirit he was of; and asked his advice with regard to my own conduct. He said, "My brother, I must first ask you one or two questions. Have you the witness within yourself? Does the Spirit of God bear witness with your spirit, that you are a child of God?" I was surprised, and knew not what to answer. He observed it, and asked, "Do you know Jesus Christ?" I paused and said, "I know He is the Saviour of the world." "True," replied he; "but do you know he has saved you?" I answered, "I hope he has died to save me."

[1] Williston Walker, *A History of the Christian Church*, Charles Scribner's Sons, New York, 1942 ed.

He only added, "Do you know yourself?" I said, "I do."
But I fear they were vain words.

The truth is that I did not want anyone—God or
man—to be sacrificed on my behalf. Lenin was agree-
able to sacrificing half the world in order to forward
his theories, but I told myself that I was not inclined to
be so free with other people's lives. The Biblical arrange-
ment by which righteousness is imputed to the believer
is wonderful, but (as I reasoned) it is too hard on the
sacrificial victim. It seemed to turn Jesus Christ into a
kind of scapegoat for a makeshift cosmic plan to gloss
over the defects of the human race, in order to satisfy
the Creator. The Cross becomes a kind of apology for
man as the one creative act that misfired. I called it un-
fair to Jesus.

Yet the answer of Scripture was that I could not
have it any other way. All the power of the Christian
life, the promise of joy beyond pain and triumph beyond
tragedy, is possible only because of those six wretched
hours on Calvary when God "made him to be sin for us,
who knew no sin; that we might be made the righteousness of God." (II Corinthians 5:21)

Today I know that the reason Christ died upon the
Cross was to ready me to meet God, here and hereafter.
The years of hunger and thirst have ended in blessedness
and the filling of the Holy Spirit. That which alienated
me from the presence of the Lord has been taken away,
removed, covered. I have freedom of access with every
other believer—as Peter Forsyth says—not because I am

a lover of love, but because I am an object of Grace. Once this tremendous truth comes home, the search is over, the seeker becomes a finder, and Christianity comes alive. When the sinner owns up to his sin and is clothed with the divine righteousness, all the dull, dreary forms of the Church become clothed in His sight with richness and glory. Life itself is transformed into a doxology. He is born anew.

5

The Making of Merciful Men

I

THE FIFTH BEATITUDE seems to offer some more straightforward "boot-strap religion." Virtue appears to be its own reward. If we are kind and forgiving toward other people, they—together with Providence—will be favorably disposed toward us. The way we treat those around us conditions the kind of clemency we receive, not only from our neighbors, but from God Himself. The Golden Rule (or a misunderstanding of it) is thus projected into outer space by a kind of celestial stimulus-response or push-button formula. If our welldoing measures up in quality, God presumably can be "triggered" into an appropriate response. Another well-known verse is often cited to underscore the point: "Forgive us our debts, as we forgive our debtors," to which is added our Lord's comment, "For if ye forgive men their trespasses, your heavenly Father will also forgive you." (Matthew 6:12, 14)

We are seeking to interpret the Beatitudes by the Cross. We are seeking the person behind the teachings, believing that in these verses portraying the blessed man, Jesus Himself is the character described. Or as Carl Henry has interpreted it, "He clothes the Beatitudes with his own life." [1]

Jesus' life, we know, derives its full meaning from the Cross. How does the Cross bear out the "stimulus-response" interpretation of the fifth Beatitude? We may begin by saying that Jesus of Nazareth was one who practiced mercy daily. "All they that had any sick . . . brought them unto him; and he laid his hands on every one of them, and healed them." (Luke 4:40) Compassion was the essence of His character. It led Him to frequent unsavory places and to touch the untouchable. It gave Him a special concern for the weak; for children, for the handicapped, for the misfits and victims of society. He refused to countenance violence or bloodshed on His behalf. Even on the Roman gallows, as the reformer Zwingli has said, our Lord was "true to Himself" and forgave those who sought to do away with Him. Yet when the sentence of man was passed upon Him, He received no clemency. His reward was neither acquittal nor pardon but execution, and there was no interference.

Here is the one stark fact about the crucifixion of Christ that stands out above all others: from every human

[1] Carl F. H. Henry, *Christian Personal Ethics,* Wm. B. Eerdmans Publishing Company, Grand Rapids, 1957.

63

point of view it was merciless. It was brought about by the two cruelest forces of the ancient world: imperial might and religious fanaticism. Roman law was inexorable. Its justice was cruel and final. The empire that systematically enslaved sixty million people was in no mood to trifle with a man who, according to his own tribe, claimed to be a rival of Caesar. As for the religious bigots of the time, they (like their counterparts today of whatever persuasion) showed a supreme inability to sympathize with or understand someone of differing views. Thus the merciful one obtained no mercy.

We are forced to go back to our Beatitude and ask, "What does it mean?" Obviously it does not mean, "Do this and you'll get that." In the storm and stress of life no sheltered island is promised where the faithful will be rewarded. A dedicated Christian friend once said in my presence, "I believe that as long as I am taking care of my orphans, the Lord will take care of me." We can admire him and love him for his compassionate heart; but what will he do with the Cross? For the Cross makes it clear that the way God takes care of us may be altogether different from the way we reward (or fail to reward) each other. If we are decent and loving to each other, we may reap thanks in this life and we may not. We may die full of years like Father Abraham and we may not. Life hands us no gilt-edged warranty that rectitude wins "the big payoff." If we look to Jesus Christ, He does not pin a "good-conduct" medal on our chests; He hands us a Cross.

"The quality of mercy," says Portia, "is not strained; it droppeth as the gentle rain from heaven." The Shakespearean figure is valid and Scriptural. It corrects the fallacy that mercy can be conjured up on earth out of a bottle or a good-will sack. Christian faith teaches that mercy does not go up that it may come down; it comes down *period*. It is unmerited favor from God Himself to an erring people who can do nothing to earn it except to hold out their hands.

When we understand that mercy follows the line of vertical descent, the fog layers of our confusion begin to burn off. There is no stimulus-response, we discover; there is no bargaining for divine favor. To make a bargain one must have something to bargain with; and if we had anything to bargain with we would not need mercy. Our repentance is no asset, for it is the liquidation of all assets. "And if by grace, then is it no more of works: otherwise grace is no more grace." (Romans 11:6) There is no "triggering" here, for God's mercy belongs to Himself and He exercises Crown rights over what is His own. We can plead and beg for mercy, but you will note that the Beatitude does not suggest we shall necessarily receive it.

What, then? Having eliminated from our quest all human impulses, prayers, sympathies, pityings, generosities, deeds, penances, sacrifices, almsgiving, self-interests, props, crutches and derring-do; having seen that none of these have any claim on the mercy of the Lord; having ascribed absolute sovereignty to God in all these matters as the sole fount of Grace, what are we to do next? What further conditions need to be fulfilled?

Let us see what the New Testament means by mercy. The word is not a synonym for charity or even for pity in its ordinary usage. Mercy is primarily the gracious act of God in dealing with men: not after their just deserts, but by releasing them, pardoning them, setting them free from the just penalty of their wrongdoings.

Mercy does not set aside justice or belittle justice. The Word of God is terrible in its promise of recompense: "Vengeance is mine; I will repay, saith the Lord!" Mercy does not minimize the offense of the Cross. "If I were God," cried Martin Luther, "and the world had treated me as it has treated Him, I would kick the wretched thing to pieces." Yet so unspeakable is the love of God that He took the penalty of our sin upon Himself, that mercy might "rejoice" over judgment (James 2:13), and the stain upon men's lives might be wiped away.

Today the earth and the skies are filled with signs that suggest not the mercy of God but rather impending doom. The race for space is just another indication that the Lord in inexorable in His judgments upon sin, and that "the way of the ungodly shall perish." It is a time when men's hearts are failing them for fear; when the imagination shrinks at the portents of the future. What should the Christian do? Should he raise children, vote for school bonds, build his church and try to live a decent life, when the Lord seems about to permit him to blast himself off the planet?

To know God is to know the answer. As the Scripture says, He is slow to anger, kind, patient, compassionate, ready to pardon, eager to impart to us the gift of Life. At the Cross love triumphed over justice in the heart of our heavenly Father, and every condition was fulfilled that was required to set men free from the power that thwarts their lives. You and I may hold back with our doubts; we may hesitate to accept God's offer of pardon and peace; but there is no straining the quality of God's mercy. All He requires is our brokenness.

To walk in that mercy is to know freedom from worry about the future, for the future lies with God. It is to know freedom from worry about the present, because each day is a walk in fellowship with our Lord. And it is to know freedom from worry about the past, because "the blood of Jesus Christ his Son cleanseth us from all sin."

3

What is a merciful man? The New Testament's answer is that he is first of all mercy-full. He is filled with the mercy of God, and in that state he is emptied of everything else, or the term means nothing. We quickly recognize that the ordinary meaning of the term "merciful" today is hardly "mercy-full," any more than "graceful" suggests in common usage "filled with the Grace of God." Yet let us reflect a moment: mercy, we said, descends from heaven as a prime attribute of God. How then can we speak of a merciful person without suggesting the fullness of God in him?

The quintessence of mercy lies in its moving beyond the nicely calculated judgments that regulate our human relationships. It transcends the strictures of justice. Perhaps a very earthy incident will illustrate the operation of free mercy in the Kingdom of God. The municipality of Richmond, California, maintains a carefully-worked-out system of traffic ordinances, with fines graded according to the seriousness of the offense. Not long ago I was stopped by a servant of that city and charged with a violation involving a fine of some twenty-seven dollars. When court convened I entered a plea of "guilty." Apart from explaining that the act was "unintentional," I made no effort to defend myself. The judge, surprisingly, set aside the hierarchy of penalties and proceeded to administer not justice but mercy. I walked out of the courtroom a defenseless violator of the law, stripped of every "extenuating circumstance" and disarmed of every rationalization, yet pardoned and filled with mercy.

Until a man has encountered the living Lord in some such way he cannot know the meaning of the word "merciful."

> Just as I am, without one plea,
> But that thy blood was shed for me,
> And that thou bidd'st me come to thee. . . .

To be merciful is to be filled with God. The eyes of compassion are not human eyes. When we look feelingly upon our brother in need, it is not our own feelings that affect us; our own feelings are quite "unfeeling." In the battle for survival it is "every man for himself" and we are quite "merciless." God pity us; we even take secret enjoyment in other people's discomfiture. When we look upon our brother in mercy, it is the Lord who looks and feels and makes use of us as His instruments, "For it is God which worketh in you both to will and to do of his good pleasure." (Philippians 2:13) Writing to a mother who had lost her child, Baron von Hügel declared, "It is He who made the mother's heart; it is not simply her love, but in the first instance His love, with just some drops of it fallen into the mother's heart. . . ." [2] Since God is the author of all mercy, every cup of cold water is really given in the name of Jesus, although only those who are in the beloved can understand the reward.

Once on a by-street in Hilo, Hawaii, I witnessed a strange sight that has haunted me since. It was a trial conducted by a flock of mynah birds. In the center of the street one forlorn bird had alighted, and in a surrounding circle several feet in diameter were fifteen or twenty of its "peers." The trial consisted of shrieking and chattering and hopping up and down. At the conclusion of the deliberations the jury pounced upon the bird in the center and pecked it to death with long, sharp beaks. Then court was adjourned and all flew into nearby trees. Shocked at this disturbance in nature, I went over and removed the body.

[2] *Essays and Addresses*, E. P. Dutton & Company, New York, 1921.

69

More than once since then I have seen men behave in ways that reminded me of a mynah-bird trial. Justice that is not tempered with mercy is perpetually in danger of becoming "mynah-bird justice."

Speaking vertically, with reference to God, no one of us can make any pretensions in the realm of mercy. We are all mynah birds at heart. We are disqualified by our very natures. We cannot administer what we do not have. Only God can make us merciful; only God is unfailing in pity and tenderness; only "his mercy endureth forever." And so great was God's love toward us that He disregarded our shortcomings, failures, and missing of the mark, and sent us a clean bill of health. He published His amnesty and established His fount of mercy on the most unlikely spot on the face of the earth: the Golgotha execution grounds. It was there, where murder was officially condoned by mankind in the name of religion and law, where imperial justice and ecclesiastical scruple had smothered every spark of human pity, that we received eternal pardon and grace.

No wonder men have been confused by the Cross! For amid all the "mynah-bird" passions at the Place of the Skull, the believing Christian has found nothing but love—love—love, and mercy surpassing all earthly thoughts and deeds. The bloodstained beams have become the precious and beautiful symbol of salvation. The whole sordid, rubbish-littered scene of Calvary has been forever transfixed with the ineffable glory of God.

> Mercy there was great, and grace was free,
> Pardon there was multiplied to me,

There my burdened soul found liberty,
At Calvary.

4

This Beatitude offers us a chance to re-examine some of the sore points in our personal lives. Perhaps we think we have treated our neighbor justly, but have we been merciful? The merciful man is the magnanimous man. He "overlooks" the wrongs that have been done him, just as God, in the words of Paul, "passed over" our former sins. (Romans 3:25) That is, the Christian hands out horizontally toward his fellow what he has received vertically from the Lord.

There are seasons when Christians are invited to make a special gift to the One Great Hour of Sharing or similar charity for the relief of the world's suffering. In our self-inventory today we are asking whether such generosity is merely applying salve to our sore consciences. It may be a different story when we are asked to be men of mercy to the Jew or the devout Roman Catholic or the man of different skin alongside us, or to the rather obnoxious alcoholic across the street, or even to the person living under the same roof with us. "You have to do a lot of business with God," says Edward John Carnell, "to mellow out in sweetness." Yet in parable after parable Jesus Christ identifies Himself with just such folk as "these my brethren."

Even if we have the good will to be merciful, and we sincerely want to be used of God as instruments of His grace, we do not always know how to proceed. Should we "tell off" a person for his own good? Is it not more merciful in some cases to be polite and tactful, and to skip the facts? Does a man achieve more under a "hardboiled" boss than under one who is gentle and "merciful"? Could there be a situation in which it would be kind to be harsh, and unkind to be kind?

Ernest Ligon, the child psychologist, suggests, "Mercy does not always express itself by withholding punishment. For one child punishment may be necessary, in another it may produce a sullen, spiritless, and antisocial personality. Permitting a youth to work his way through college may develop a sense of responsibility in one student, produce an overmaterialistic, money-grabbing philosophy of life in another, and an inferiority complex in a third." [3]

If it takes wisdom to establish justice, it takes even more to have mercy; in fact, it takes more than man possesses. Without the guidance of the Holy Spirit the Christian hardly knows how to begin to act. The making of merciful men is a divine art. If there is any one rule that can be given, it is, "Follow Jesus Christ."

A friend of mine recently returned from a trip to South America where he investigated the state of the Church. He discovered that everywhere the Pentecostal movement is making strides, and he inquired of the nationals and missionaries he met the reason for their advance. They told him, "The Pentecostals are accepted because they believe that *Jesus has the answer to every*

[3] Ernest Ligon, *The Psychology of Christian Personality*, The Macmillan Company, New York, 1935.

problem." Certainly in the matter of mercy we can trust Jesus. He was not soft as mush, He was hard as steel. The sternest words in the Bible are not found in the Old Testament, they are found on the lips of Jesus; yet His life was a symphony of mercy.

He teaches us that the merciful man is the one who seeks to save others from suffering, even at the cost of immediate pain, and even if it means vicarious suffering on his own part. From Jesus we gather that the merciful man does not seek to improve his own status at the expense of the misery of his fellow. He leaves practical jokes to others. He has a compassionate heart. He goes the second mile. He brushes off the slights and buffets that come his way as of little consequence. In all these things he anticipates no reward, but simply conforms in obedience to the pattern of his Master.

In the tabernacle of the ancient Hebrews the center of worship was the Mercy Seat, over which brooded the cherubim with wings outstretched above the Ark of the Covenant. When the veil of the temple was torn in two at the time of the Crucifixion, Jesus Christ became our Mercy Seat. It is from that Seat that our Lord creates the man of mercy. He does not promise such a man that he shall have "self-fulfillment" as our culture understands it, or even that he shall be "happy," as some translators interpret the first word of our Beatitude.

Nevertheless Jesus Christ does promise a blessing and it is this: open access to all the riches of heaven. To "obtain mercy" is not only to receive a passport to immortality; it is to unlock the door to life's greatest mystery

73

and its most elusive, guarded secret. What the artist dreams of in his cubes and abstractions, what the alchemist searched for in his magic elixir, what the playboy seeks in his ritual of sex, what the manager pursues in his disappearing "plateau" of success is what the Lord Jesus Christ issues as standard equipment for those who are His own: *peace with joy* in the borrowed dimensions of mercy.

5

To read the New Testament is to realize that we are not just saved *from* something but *for* something. God's purpose in accomplishing our salvation was, after all, to make us useful to Himself. We are newly "created in Christ Jesus unto good works"; and those works are, broadly speaking, works of mercy. By now it should be evident that our Beatitude is not so much a statement of cause and effect as it is an equation. It could be equally well stated in reverse: "Blessed are they that obtain mercy: for they shall be merciful." Our Lord said something very much like it in Luke's account of the Sermon on the Plain: "Be ye therefore merciful, as your Father also is merciful." (Luke 6:36)

The same kind of equation is evident in the verse, "Forgive us our debts, as we forgive our debtors." It is not simply cause and effect ("If ye forgive men their trespasses, your heavenly Father will also forgive you"), for it also works in reverse: "Be ye kind . . . forgiving one another, even as God for Christ's sake hath forgiven you." (Ephesians 4:32) The whole earth is filled with

74

the mercy of God. We love our fellow human beings because He first loved us (I John 4:19), but we also love them in order that we might love God better (I John 4:20). Our works of mercy do not earn our fare to heaven, they are simply the staple diet of the Christian life. As the practical proverb puts it, "The merciful man doeth good to his own soul." (Proverbs 11:17)

The world desperately needs to learn that Jesus went to the Cross to create a race of new men—merciful men. It needs these men, for our human race is perishing for lack of love and mercy. We may have thought once that we were outgrowing the cruelties of the ancients and the "barbarians," but we have been rudely awakened. The latest revolution in Cuba uncovered the same brutal tortures that were used in primeval Egypt and Phoenicia. God is weary of our inhumanities. He is looking for this new race to assert itself: men who will take Jesus Christ seriously, men of mercy, who are willing to make the same kind of absolute sacrifice in His name and in our time. Such men He will use mightily.

A debate is being waged around the world today over the words "justice" and "democracy." Our nation is committed to its hard-won convictions; we will part with them dearly indeed. However, in other parts of the world we are told that our democracy is not pure, and that our freedom is not freedom at all. Many of our difficulties are semantic. There is tremendous confusion simply over words.

It is not so with regard to mercy. Its meaning is changeless. There is no mistaking the cry of a ragged, starving child, or the timid handclasp of the friendless and downtrodden. Need speaks a universal language and hunger knows no iron curtain. We never seem to run out of the demands of mercy, for the tyrant is always at hand, and no immigration statutes seem to keep out the oppressor of the poor. The beggars with their sores were pitiful in Jesus' day, but the suffering and homelessness of thousands and even millions in our time are more poignant because our nations possess the technical ability to relieve the condition.

There is indescribable poverty in this year of Grace in Korea, in Hong Kong, in Jordan, in India, in Africa, but we need not go so far afield. Within a dozen miles of where you live there is destitution that you never suspected was there. Visit a city rescue mission and let life speak to you.

John R. Mott once described the call of God in a man's life as "the recognition of a need and the capacity to meet that need." We who go by the name of Christ and who see the need have a task that is herculean. We dwell in a century which, whatever else it may be called, will never be known as the "Century of Mercy." Its latest tragic development is the emergence of Communist "assistance to backward nations." The merciless are now simulating mercy, not out of love for the brethren but in order to propagandize an appeal for world domination.

Our Western leaders are being told that they must quickly extend a helping hand to the world's wretched or fall before the power of a dictatorship. Frank Laubach says, "The United States must make an all-out effort to help the destitute half of the world out of its misery, or we shall find that the world has gone Communist because of our neglect." His entreaty is based on absolute truth, but it will be ignored. Fear has never yet begotten mercy and kindness. Only Christians who know the perfect love that casts out fear can act with what Samuel Hopkins called "disinterested benevolence." With the New Testament as their guide, they must take the lead in teaching the world the sincere brotherly concern and humanity that is the stamp of the Savior on a man's life.

Our Beatitude is more than an equation; it is an intersection, a meeting of the vertical with the horizontal. That mercy which "droppeth as the gentle rain from heaven" covers the earth with streams of living water. The free Grace of God becomes a human commodity, not for profit but for blessing in the everyday encounters of life. The very things which, we said earlier, could not incite the mercy of God toward us become the vehicles whereby we are to express God's love and compassion: our sympathies, pityings, generosities, deeds, sacrifices, and charity. The divine forgiveness, by which we are "accepted in the beloved," is mediated through us as a means of reconciling man with man.

6

The Washing of the Cup

I

THE DISCIPLINE of Scripture is bringing us into the very center of the laboratory of life. In eleven short words Jesus now faces us with man's highest hope and his deepest frustration. The longing within the human breast to behold the face of God is primordial. We yearn to leap over the barriers of sense and time and look full front upon Him who fashioned us. Yet something within rebuffs us—slaps us down—with the knowledge that we are morally unfit for such an experience. Our myopic vision will not reach to the far ranges of eternity. Its white radiance is too much for us. God is holy, and we are soiled and puny.

"Who shall ascend into the hill of the Lord?" asks the Psalmist, "Or who shall stand in his holy place? He that hath clean hands, and a pure heart." Where does

78

that leave us, who are confronted with our imperfections night and day? Are we doomed never to see the face of God? Is Jesus Christ holding out before us a flying goal, a carrot on the end of a stick? Surely our Lord would be cruel to promise us the vision of heaven through the achievement of personal purity, knowing all the time that we could never achieve it. There are no glad tidings here.

Perhaps you are inclined to point out that, while you are admittedly imperfect, there are many who are morally inferior and considerably more delinquent than you. In fact, all things taken into view, you rank rather high in the scale of human behavior. We seem always so much more willing to confess the sins of others than to recognize our own! But let it be clear that Jesus is not promising the vision of God to those who may be relatively better than others. He is talking about *purity*, which is an absolute and not a relative condition. Only the pure in heart will be blessed and shall see God.

Dr. Jung, the Swiss psychologist, believes that each of us wears a *persona*, which in Latin means "mask," and that our *persona* is really the "person" we present to the public view. Our inner thoughts we prefer to conceal; we even seek to hide them from ourselves. We demurely convey the impression that we are moral, law-abiding citizens while our imaginations run riot. Our bookshelves present the staid classics—but what is that dog-eared volume hidden behind? Some of us like to carry ourselves as if we were Sir Galahad, who declared in the lines of the Victorian poet,

> My strength is as the strength of ten,
> Because my heart is pure.

The truth is that we are better compared to Sir Lancelot, who carried himself nobly and wielded his sword valorously, but who while he fought betrayed the lord he served.

If only we can bring ourselves to face our impurity, there is hope for us. If only we can stand the thought that we are not good enough for God, we have a chance. We need major cardiac surgery of the kind that the Lord prescribed for Israel: "A new heart also will I give you, and a new spirit will I put within you: and I will take away the stony heart out of your flesh, and I will give you an heart of flesh." (Ezekiel 36:26) The old heart must go, for it was impure. With a new heart, shall we be able to see our Lord?

Let us look again at the words of the twenty-fourth Psalm, third and fourth verses:

> Who shall ascend into the hill of the Lord? or who shall stand in his holy place? He that hath clean hands, and a pure heart; who hath not lifted up his soul unto vanity, nor sworn deceitfully.

A question is asked and an answer given. Let us ask whether the reverse is also true. Perhaps if we deduce the opposite question and a corresponding answer we may learn something:

> Who shall be struck down upon the hill of the Lord? or who shall fall in his holy place? He that hath unclean hands, and an impure heart; who hath lifted up his soul unto vanity, and sworn deceitfully.

What is this but a picture of man—not as he ought to be but as he is? The twisted verses reflect the whole history of nations and civilizations and tell the fate of humanity. They pinpoint the bullying child, the mother who exploits her family to further her ambition, the man who spends his leisure scheming to magnify his importance, the dictator with a global power complex. All these are guilty of "lifting up their soul unto vanity."

But there is something curious about this perverted Scripture. It is inaccurate. Who was it that was struck down upon the hill of the Lord? Jesus Christ, the only one whose hands were clean and conscience sound. The innocent took the place of the guilty, the just of the unjust. His crucifixion on Calvary meant that He deliberately sacrificed His purity on our behalf, that we might be rendered fit to see God. The Great Physician performed a Good Friday operation to remove the stone and to graft in the gift of life: a new, pure heart.

The Beatitude brings us a great hope: that because He lived we too shall live and shall see the face of God. He has made clear the way: we are to take up our crosses and follow the path to that same hill where we also must climb and be struck down and crucified with Him.

2

Purity of heart requires the purity of Christ, and that is, first of all, not so much spotlessness as integrity. Forty-seven times in the Fourth Gospel Jesus declared that what He did was not done by His will alone but by the will of the Father. Because He was absolutely certain at the point of motivation, Jesus had no fears as to the consequences. They could call Him a consorter with sinners and winebibbers, it did not matter. For Him separation was a matter of vocation rather than location.

The integrity Christ taught was not something built up over a period of years like a credit rating, or an award for safe driving. Such matters are established by the absence of stain on the record. The pure heart is more like an unexpected gift suddenly placed in the hands. Its chief characteristic is not the absence of flaws but openness toward the giver.

In Scripture one of the clearest symbols of the believer is the vessel or cup. A Christian is a cup filled to overflowing with the water of life. He himself is an "earthen" vessel—dirt—but the water purifies and sanctifies the vessel as long as it is being poured in. When the water's flow is stopped the cup becomes stale and stagnant. The two chief marks of the cup are that it has the capacity to contain and is open at the top. Capacity is what we bring to God—and it is all we bring. Openness is what makes possible purity, as the riches of glory are poured into the vessels of mercy.

As long as the divine life is being poured into our hearts we have a chance to see ourselves as God sees us. Therein lies our hope; for when we seek to examine ourselves "objectively" we engage in a vast self-deception. Our blacks become grays or else disappear entirely. We may become meticulously honest at one point but we ignore three others. We say we detest hypocrites, that we would far rather be condemned as sinners than as two-faced pretenders, yet even in the midst of our protestation we are artfully weaving a tapestry of hypocrisy. On the tapesty is a legend which, when translated, suggests that not only do we intend to have our cake, but we will eat it too. If we cannot call ourselves pure in heart, at least no man dare call us impure, for how can one see in when the shades are drawn? Thus the sediment collects in the bottom of our cup and renders it unfit for use.

Only when God's living water is splashing in the cup can it be clean. Purity of heart then becomes no longer a conscious state at all, but an unconscious one. When a mother is busy training her child in his proper duties she does not ask herself, "Am I a good mother?" The very activity in which she is engaged answers the question. When a Christian is laboring in his vocation his virtue is absorbed in his work.

When Jesus told the Parable of the Last Judgment (Matthew 25), He described how the righteous ones would be rewarded because they fed Him when He was hungry, and quenched His thirst, and gave Him a home, and clothed Him, and visited Him in distress. Then Jesus pictured them as reacting in surprise and asking when they had ever done these things: "Lord, when saw we thee an hungred, and fed thee? or thirsty, and gave thee drink? When saw we thee a stranger, and took thee in? or naked, and clothed thee? Or when saw we thee sick, or in prison, and came unto thee?" (Matthew 25:37-39) That for which they were being rewarded was done unconsciously as the overflow of a God-filled life. The pure heart does not know that it is acting purely, it only knows that it is responding to the Spirit.

The only conscious thing we can say about the pure

in heart is that they are fundamentally honest about their own impurity. They are not "kidding" themselves. They have carried motivation research to the point where they know that since the "heart is deceitful above all things" (Jeremiah 17:9), the good life must be a gift of Grace, and their good works are but the works of the Lord. This frankness and honesty is the basis of Christian integrity. It is grounded at the Cross, where everything is level. It provides a framework of human nothingness from which a man can look out and see the face of God.

3

In his biography of one of the leaders of the Reformation, Samuel Macaulay Jackson notes that in his early years Zwingli did not preach the Gospel in its fullness, as he was involved in a licentious sex relationship. The biographer adds significantly, "Blessed are the pure in heart: for they shall see God."

This Beatitude has always focused a searchlight on the struggle of Spirit against flesh. Purity of heart and lust will not be bedfellows. From the human point of view, of course, there is simply no contest, for our bodily nature has drives so strong that they clamor for our complete attention. Flesh triumphs. A hundred times a day—or is it a thousand?—we receive sexual stimuli from all kinds of sources, and far too often the effect is to provoke reflections that lead to impurity of heart.

The famed ascetic Jerome, who wrestled for years with his soul in solitude and fasting, far removed from all outward temptations of the flesh, reports that he was still plagued by visions of bevies of dancing maidens. The way of asceticism will put iron in the soul, but it will not remove the impurity. All the virtuous resolutions in the world will not purge a man. Benjamin Franklin in his youth made a list of puritan virtues that he resolved to achieve. At the very time he was punctiliously endeavoring to observe them, he was engaged in a shabby pursuit of sex in London.

Jesus had a number of things to say about the sexual behavior of men and women, but His sociology, like His physical therapy, always occupied a secondary position. Christ's greater concern was to show that the Spirit of God could do for man what he could not do for himself: win victory over his body. Only God is the creator of flesh and only God is stronger than flesh; but He joins battle on this ground only on behalf of those who are willing to receive purity on His conditions.

What are the conditions? They are very simple. First, we are to recognize that God made flesh in the first place, and there is nothing inherently evil or shameful about it. All the works of the Lord are good; "there is nothing unclean of itself." (Romans 14:14) The original sin committed in Eden was neither lust nor greed, but pride.

Nevertheless a blight has fallen upon mankind which we Christians call sin, and this blight has created disorder in man's sexual pattern as well as in other areas of his life. The rape in the park, the incident that created gossip next door, the statistics of the Kinsey Report are all symptoms of the dislocation in what the New

Testament calls "the flesh." No man ever finds God working in his body until he first finds the moral taint and impurity in his body.

The third condition God requires is that a man invite Him to come in and possess his body. The body then becomes a temple of the Holy Spirit (I Corinthians 6:19), and the owner of the body becomes a new man in Jesus Christ.

Let it not be imagined that this new man is a kind of "superman" endowed with tremendous ability that enables him to get self-mastery over the flesh and to develop into some sort of spiritual giant. There is no such thing as a victorious Christian, there is only a victorious Christ. There are no conquests of the "new man" over the "old man," for the Christian is just as weak after he has been translated into the Kingdom of God as he was before. He is, in fact, weaker, for now he is fully aware of his weakness and knows that he dare make "no provision for the flesh." The impurities that he formerly took as a matter of course in his daily walk—the continual flaunting of flesh for commercial purposes, the inevitable round of sex stories—now sear his soul and make him realize he is a pilgrim and a stranger on the earth. They test his strength and find it wanting, and cause him to lean more and more on the only source of his spiritual strength, the Lord Jesus Christ.

We do not move from "dirty" thoughts to pure thoughts by seeking to get closer to the Lord—for example, by attending church more regularly. Demons are not exorcised by sacred organ music. Every church has its share of impurity of heart. A man's life becomes pure only when God takes complete control of it and begins thinking His thoughts through the man's mind. For when the Lord moves, He brings His purity with Him and even the flesh is hallowed by the gracious presence of Deity.

4

In a church where I once ministered, some young people came to me after the service of Holy Communion and expressed unhappiness with the way it had been conducted.

"What was wrong?" I asked.

"We didn't like your suggestion that we took part because we were perfect or something. We don't feel like that."

I went over the service and soon found the part that dissatisfied them. It read:

> Ye who do truly and earnestly repent of your sins, and are in love and charity with your neighbors, and intend to lead a new life, following the commandments of God, and walking from henceforth in His holy ways: Draw near with faith, and take this Holy Sacrament to your comfort; and make your humble confession to Almighty God.

Teen-age honesty had rebelled at words and phrases that suggested a purity of heart they did not feel. I now use another form of invitation to the Sacrament. In a sense there is nothing wrong with the traditional words;

they are a sincere attempt to describe the pure intent without which, said Jesus, no man shall see God. My young friends had found nevertheless that the words were meaningless to them.

In Edinburgh I heard the story of a venerable Scottish divine who was sitting in a pew during the service of Holy Communion. At this service the elements were passed, and he noticed that a girl in front of him refused the bread when it came to her, and that she was weeping. While the usher hesitated the old man leaned forward and whispered, "Take it, lassie. It's for sinners!"

Surely this is the Gospel, that while we were yet sinners Christ died for us. But were not the honest teenagers right? And was not the Scottish "lassie" obeying a true instinct? Does God invite the unholy to lay hands upon pure and holy things? "There is no difference," replies Paul, "all have sinned, and come short of the glory of God." In other words, in the Lord's sight one man is as bad as another. But if that be true, let us argue, is it not a little irrelevant to talk about the "pure in heart" seeing God? And why does the Communion service contain the prayer: ". . . that, drawing near unto Thee with a pure heart and conscience undefiled, we may receive these Thy gifts without sin. . . ."

If we look to the Cross we see the answer etched boldly against the sky. Purity of heart is from beyond ourselves. We are made worthy of the Communion table neither by washing our hands of the past nor by resolving to do better in the future. We were "prepared" for Communion two thousand years ago by the very act

88

which Communion recalls—the body of Christ broken upon the Cross for us, the blood of Christ poured out upon the ground for us. What my young people did not understand is that the sacrament is a means of Grace, and that through God's Grace they may *receive* newness of life as an unearned gift.

What a relief it is to know that even though it is hopeless to try to clean up our lives and so fit them for God, cleansing is still possible. All we need to do is to turn our hearts over to Him. "Purge me . . . and I shall be clean: wash me, and I shall be whiter than snow." (Psalm 51:7) The old minister spoke truth: the Communion service itself brings the conditions for Communion. The unholy hand becomes holy when it takes the sacred bread: not because the bread contains a "spiritual vitamin" or imparts some purifying quality, but because God loves sinners and gave His Son for them.

Unless we give the Father His Crown rights in the matter, and ascribe everything to the divine initiative, this Beatitude will never permit us to see our Lord. It will only confuse and discourage us. The Communion service will then become just another moral wrestling bout. The "joy of the believer" will disappear as the X-ray of truth is trained upon our sinful conscience. We will give up and let someone else sing the praises of Zion, for we are too wicked. Someone else can be in Wesley Nelson's phrase, a "prayed-up, Bible-loving, God-honoring, fully-consecrated, victorious-living, witnessing, successful soul-winning Christian." We will sneak into the rear pew and see if we cannot "just make it in." How many church members have resigned themselves to just this kind of dismal Christianity? Here is a fair bed of spikes indeed, a paradox of hopeful hopelessness.

When we give God the glory, everything changes. He becomes the purifying agent, and we see that our part is confession through self-criticism. "Let a man examine himself," said Paul, "and so let him eat of that bread, and drink of that cup." (I Corinthians 11:28) The Scottish girl's tears did not prove that her heart was either pure or impure. They proved only that she was in communion with the One who purifies, and that her conscience was—to use the old phrase—"under conviction."

We need to confess our sins if we want them forgiven. The purpose of confession is not to purify but to purge. Evangelical Christians are frequently guilty of self-delusion at this point. We emphasize the need to "confess our sins to God alone" but we seldom bother to do it. The result is that the psychiatrist has become the "Protestant confessor." Scriptural teaching provides the solution: "Confess your faults one to another, and pray one for another, that ye may be healed." (James 5:16) A Christian brother or sister only distantly related to our daily orbit can be of vast assistance in bringing us to examine ourselves before God.

Though the confession does not purify, the forgiveness of God does. As the prophet Isaiah sang, "He will have mercy . . . and . . . abundantly pardon," and as John cast it in New Testament metal, "The blood of Jesus Christ his Son cleanseth us from all sin."

90

5

"For they shall *see God.*"

How is it possible? Scripture declares emphatically that "no man hath seen God at any time"; for He is described as "dwelling in light which no man can approach unto" (I Timothy 6:16). The experience of mankind would seem to verify the point. Neither history nor science knows of a visible God. If we shatter the atom into a billion fragments, or send a space expedition to the farthest star, or dig up every archaeological artifact beneath the earth's crust, we shall be no whit closer to the face of Deity: this we know. A good thing it is, for the thought of a direct encounter with the sovereign majesty of the Lord, the architect of the universe, is—apart from His love—enough to strike the imagination with terror.

How is it, then, that in the face of all this evidence Jesus can utter the quite simple statement that those whose hearts are pure shall see the Lord?

Did He mean it?

How did He mean it? Symbolically?

We could suppose that He has given us a figure of speech, to teach us that if we were very, very good we would be rewarded with a warm and pious kind of feeling.

Or we could get rid of the difficulty by classifying it as an "eschatological" statement, stating that what Jesus was talking about was God in the hereafter, not here and now.

Both suggestions, of course, draw the teeth of the Beatitude.

There is no question that Jesus meant what He said. He always did. He was not implying that the blessings of this Beatitude, or any of the Beatitudes, would be stored up for distribution in some future life rather than in the present. His teaching, like His healing, had immediate relevance. Whatever experience the "pure in heart" were to have, they were to have it now as well as later.

But what experience? To think of seeing God as an "experience" is perhaps to think of visions. When we open this door but a crack, what a host of shapes come tumbling in: hallucinations, apparitions, spooks, flying saucers, demons, gremlins, psycho-kinetic energy, extrasensory perception, mental illness, mass psychosis, optical illusions, pathological delusions, projections, psychic phenomena, "contact with the unseen world," et cetera, et cetera. Where is the beginning and where the ending, and which way leads to God?

Jesus had a very plain answer. It is not the development of some occult sense that brings us face to face with the living Lord. Jesus does not even use that door. He does not tell us where it leads. He points instead to another door which has on it three words: "Truth, Goodness, Beauty." He makes it clear that the new door is the door to the Throne Room. It is the door of the pure heart. Its shape is a Cross.

Some years ago Bishop Kenneth Kirk of England wrote a beautiful book entitled *The Vision of God*, a scholarly and exhaustive treatment of the whole range of mystical experience. It leaves one amazed at the variety of ways in which men have sought to come into personal confrontation with God. They have searched in caves, in deserts, on pillars, on remote islands, in jungles, on mountain peaks. They have sat, kneeled, stood, lain prostrate, swung from ropes; they have fasted and undergone all manner of deprivation and self-inflicted punishment, all for the sight of God. "When thou saidst, Seek ye my face; my heart said unto thee, Thy face, Lord, will I seek." (Psalm 27:8)

Yet here is the answer, sweet and clear as a mountain stream: "Blessed are the pure in heart: for they shall see God." Not just the pure mind, not just the pure body is blessed, but the pure heart which governs both mind and body. The heart is the seat of affection and compassion. What Christ is telling us is that love is the way to God: suffering love that is not drowned in the deep fat of selfish considerations—pure, outgoing love, that loves for the sake of the thing loved, as a man loves his country, as a woman loves her child, as Christ loved us from the Cross.

But to *see* God there is yet another step. To find it let us turn to the story of Job: "I have heard of thee by the hearing of the ear: but now mine eye seeth thee. Wherefore I abhor myself, and repent in dust and ashes." (Job 42:5–6) Job suggests that it is not finally a veil that hides the face of the Lord from us, but our own bulky shape. We block ourselves from God's view. The moment our ego collapses and we cease to kick against the pricks, we see the Lord Jesus Christ, and "he that hath seen me hath seen the Father." The instant that the Christian life ceases to be a pilgrimage of sacred events and becomes a consuming fire, the celestial vision is ours, though there is nothing left of us but ashes. God loves ashes. They are pure. He reveals Himself to our ashes. He blows His Spirit through them and we are lost— scattered through the earth as dust—but forever His. Each burned-out flake becomes the seed of a new and pure creation.

BLESSED ARE THE PEACEMAKERS:

FOR THEY SHALL BE CALLED THE CHILDREN OF GOD.

7

Unearthly Peace

I

ONE DAY as I walked through the crowded streets of Edinburgh I came upon two small boys fighting. The fists were tiny but were doing severe damage. The onlookers were curious but passive. I stepped between the lads and asked in my alien accent, "Why are you fighting?" A stream of braid Scots issued from both mouths simultaneously and incomprehensibly (to me). "If I gave each of you a penny," I asked, "would you stop?" They nodded eagerly. With some solemnity I handed out the coins and stipulated, "Now shake hands with one another." Instead they fell into each other's arms and went frisking down the street, leaving me to reflect uneasily upon the ethics of my action.

Peacemaking is a divine activity according to Jesus. But does peacemaking consist in breaking up fights with bribes or compromises or cajolings or threats of force? Is there some other meaning to our Beatitude that does not appear upon the surface? Is our Lord saying "Well done" to my little intervention in Edinburgh, or is there a more profound theological significance to peacemaking that needs to be brought to light? It was evident to me at the time that something was missing. I had gone the first mile and had stopped the "war," but I had not really made peace, I had only bought an armistice.

Jesus says that there is a second mile; that God never intended to leave us clinging to the Cross. Good Friday leads to Easter. The Resurrection is ours also. We have "the sentence of death in ourselves" (II Corinthians 1:9) only in order that we may be delivered to a new life of righteousness and usefulness in Christ. The fruit of righteousness, according to James, is first sown by the peacemakers (3:18). To live the Christian life, then, is to follow peacemaking, and we had better find out what the Beatitude means.

Does it mean we are to seek disarmament in the world? Are we to bend our energies toward pacts in the Middle East, the reunification of Germany, the abandonment of nuclear and missile development, coexistence with Communism and the strengthening of the United Nations? Certainly it means this: that before a man can make peace with anyone, he must first establish peace with God and with himself.

Let us go back to what we discovered earlier: that the Beatitudes are not simply platitudes and axioms of virtuous behavior. They are really descriptions of Jesus

Christ. What He taught, He lived and was. In discussing the peacemaker Christ is first of all painting a portrait of Himself, and then depicting the "blessed" in whom His Spirit dwells. He is not only the Prince of Peace (Isaiah 9:6), He *is* our Peace (Ephesians 2:14). Yet He deliberately chose not to set Himself up as an arbitrator or umpire between men, such as we might expect a peacemaker to be ("Who made me a judge or a divider over you?" [Luke 12:14]).

The very expression "peacemaker" is a curious one. Edward L. R. Elson, in a sermon preached before the Queen of England and the President of the United States, suggested that in this Beatitude Jesus did not extend the blessing to include the peaceful, the peace-lovers, the peaceable, the peace-speakers, peace-wishers, or pacifists. He blessed the peace-*makers*. But the maker of peace is not the one who merely steps between two fighters. The maker of peace is the one who brings about reconciliation. The Treaty of Versailles was not peace, nor was the truce of Panmunjom. In all the history of the human race there has been only one real peace treaty. That was at Calvary, where "God was in Christ, reconciling the world unto himself." There was peace; all else has been but a confusion of bloody battles with occasional truces, armistices, and pauses for breath and ammunition.

Jesus Christ brings peace through the Cross. He reconciles man to Himself, and He reconciles men with each other and He reconciles all to God. He restores the divine fellowship that was broken by our stubbornness, fear and pride. He reaches out with a love that saves, and bids us take hold. He removes our guilt and nullifies the sentence by proclaiming an amnesty. "Turn in your weapons and go home," He says, "The battle is over. Peace has been declared."

Obviously the peace of Jesus is not something that is related directly to the agenda of some "summit meeting." Such meetings remain important; we have our "first-mile" obligation to do all that we can as good citizens to *live peaceably with all men.* Yet Jesus Christ always goes beyond to the "second mile," which is above and beyond the call of duty. His will is not simply to stop nuclear testing, or segregation; His will is to bring in the whole Kingdom of God through sacrifice.

The true peacemaker is not just the discriminating voter, not just the citizen who breaks up quarrels or the statesman who quells aggression by stripping nations of their war potential. The true peacemaker is the reconciler who offers his own life for the peace of the brethren, and whose own peace pact was signed at a "summit meeting" on a hill outside Jerusalem.

2

Robert E. Fitch has given us an interesting definition of a pietist. A pietist (whether in religion or science), he says, is one who proposes simple solutions to complex problems, who sees all issues naïvely and out of context, and who makes absolute moral judgments when the need is for compromise and adjustment. And he adds that if the pietist is allowed to have his way, he will either purge the world or destroy it.

The astonishing fact about this statement is that it fits the New Testament description of Jesus Christ. The Gospels tell us of a Man who is simple, naïve, and absolute in matters of faith and conduct. He cuts through the snarl of our ambiguities as Alexander severed the Gordian knot. "Have salt in yourselves," He says, "and have peace one with another." (Mark 9:50) Thus He disposes of the whole war question from Galilee to the moon. Imperialism? Race? Economic dislocation? Bombs? Refugees? He leaves no blueprints and establishes no principles except two: "Love God" and "Love your neighbor."

It is time for us to ask, therefore, what kind of peacemaker Jesus Christ is. His words are well known: "Peace I leave with you, my peace I give unto you; not as the world giveth, give I unto you." (John 14:27) It is obvious that He is not speaking of world peace, but what other kind of peace is there? How is it made? And what good is it?

Let us take another look at the Beatitude: "Blessed are the peacemakers: for they shall be called *the children of God*," or to speak more exactly, "*the sons of God.*" No other Beatitude has quite the same ending; our Lord must have had a special reason for choosing it. Like father, like son. Peacemakers are called sons of God because they resemble their Father, who must therefore be The Peacemaker. What Jesus is suggesting, then, is

99

"Blessed be God the Father, who makes peace, and blessed are all who follow His divine pattern."

All through Scripture there are overtones and nuances that reflect the godly origin of peace. To Isaiah God is most explicit: "I am the Lord, . . . I make peace." (45:5, 7) Jeremiah declares that not only does He make peace, He breaks it: "I have taken away my peace from this people, saith the Lord." (16:5) Peace comes through the sanctuary, says Haggai: "I will fill this house with glory . . . and in this place will I give peace, saith the Lord of hosts." (2:7, 9) Paul strengthens the unilateral view of peace-making: "Therefore being justified by faith, we have peace with God through our Lord Jesus Christ." (Romans 5:1) When we settle accounts with God, when we "make our peace" with Him, says the apostle, it is really the Lord who makes His peace with us—through Jesus Christ.

There is no use trying to resolve the paradox. On the shadow side of salvation it always seems as if we are doing it all; we groan and pray and strain after the Lord. But on the sunlit side it is always God, God all the way, God who "separated me from my mother's womb," God whose Holy Spirit draws men to Him in His own time, and who has been in complete command from the start.

If the world does not know peace today it is because it does not know God. Millions of young Americans and Europeans and Asians are being taught daily that it is quite impossible to believe in God. He is "no longer a useful hypothesis." He is the "opiate of the people." He is "a projection of the father-complex." He is a supernatural gimmick invented to keep society within bounds. He is an outmoded etiological configuration belonging to the childhood of the race. He is an artifact in the museum of the department of anthropology. God, said Nietzsche, is dead.

How tragic to grow up thus educated—to live in delusion and to die without hope! What are we Christians doing about it? Shall we wait until the Iron Curtain is melted to proclaim, "But now is Christ risen from the dead"?

Let us take heart; it is Nietzsche who is dead, not God. We know our Lord to be a living Lord because we have received His Spirit, and we know He is the Author of Peace because of the words of Jesus Christ: "These things I have spoken unto you, that in me ye might have peace." (John 16:33) It may well be peace in the midst of tribulation, it may be the hush at the vortex of a tornado, but it is still a peace that passes all understanding.

Jesus foresaw not world peace but wars and rumors of war. The New Testament pictures of the end of things are not gentle. We are reminded again of Robert Fitch's prophetic words, "If the pietist is allowed to have his way, he will either purge the world or destroy it." Jesus Christ the Peacemaker will not need to destroy the world, of course; it is increasingly evident that apart from God the world will destroy itself. Bertrand Russell says that if we do not solve our problems there is a fifty-fifty chance that not a human being will be left on the planet in forty years. So little time for the purging of the sons of peace. It is time to respond—to act!

He has sounded forth the trumpet that shall never call retreat,
He has sifted out the hearts of men before his judgment seat;
O be swift my soul to answer him, be jubilant, my feet. . . .

3

While serving as an air force chaplain during World War II I happened to pick up a little book by a Hebrew chaplain explaining the Passover to Jewish soldiers. The writer, I recall, made an earnest effort to interpret the tragedy of war and suffering in our century within a religious framework. He used words akin to these: "You will discover inevitably in life that the innocent must suffer for the guilty. Such is the way to peace. But instead of its being all wrong, it is the answer to everything. The secret of life is sacrifice." Without realizing it the rabbi was preaching the Cross of Jesus Christ, for on His Cross the innocent was sacrificed for the guilty, and became our peace.

It is possible during the reading of these pages that we have found the Christian faith presented differently from what we supposed it to be. We may have thought of it as a kind of cultural tonic or perhaps an individual morale builder. We know better now. We realize that to go through the gates of Jerusalem is to go straight to our own crucifixion. There is no way around the Cross for a Christian, no way under and no way over; but there is a way through.

We are studying a Beatitude about peace. The peace that Jesus gives is a peace with a price on it, and the price is the cost of sacrifice. Isaiah says, "the chastisement of *our* peace was upon *him*." And Paul explains: "For it pleased the Father that in him should all fulness dwell; and, having made peace through the blood of the cross, by him to reconcile all things unto himself." (Isaiah 53:5, Colossians 1:19–20) God having purchased peace for us at so great a price—the suffering of His innocent Son on behalf of the guilty—now presents us with His peace terms: unconditional surrender.

There is always a temptation to make a kind of festival out of Palm Sunday. If only Jesus Christ had ridden a white charger instead of a donkey into Jerusalem, we think. There are grounds for believing that the "triumphal entry" of Jesus Christ into the Holy City was actually a very small affair; a scattering of children and curious adults, a handful of dusty peasants in from the country, some disorganized singing, a few palm branches and a donkey ridden by an itinerant prophet.

If you would watch a triumphal procession you must turn to Roman, not Hebrew history. Rome developed the triumph to its ultimate art. The returning conqueror, the general–consul–war hero, would wait outside the city gates with his troops until invited in by the Senate. Then, after some sixty-thousand couches had lined the streets, he would make his entrance. First would come the lictors bearing the fasces, then the magistrates of the city, then the trumpeters, then the spoils—the standards, the statues, the loot, running as high as seventy-five million dollars in treasure—then the white oxen prepared for the sacrifice, and the royal prisoners (Pompey brought 322 princes), then the victorious general clad in purple and gold, seated in a chariot drawn by four horses, and followed by all his soldiers shouting *"Io triumphe!"*

How mean our Lord's entry into Jerusalem seems alongside such a display! And it was to come to an even meaner end. For this same Rome that welcomed the Caesars so lavishly was to strip Jesus of Nazareth of the only robe He had, and submit Him to the treatment reserved for its most contemptuous criminals. Christ's Palm Sunday entry did not bring Him clattering through the public square to the palace steps, there to receive the accolades of the weeping populace and the tributes of royalty. Rather it brought Him to the lash and the nails and the cry of dereliction: "My God, my God, why hast thou forsaken me?"

The peace of Jesus Christ is not the peace of the conqueror, it is the peace of the loser in this life. The heroes of Rome found that their garlands wilted quickly and their victories ended in bitterness. Not so our Lord! Jesus Christ became a victim that He might become the eternal Victor. Thus when we sign God's peace conditions in His Name we have lost, we have surrendered command of our lives; but because of the vicarious sacrifice of Christ we receive the Holy Spirit of God who raises the dead. Out of the fellowship of Christ's sufferings comes the power of the Resurrection. Not by the might of the legions, not by the power of the atom, but *by my Spirit,* says the Lord.

4

Nearly twenty years ago I lost my heart to a river, but in return it gave to me something I have treasured ever since—peace. Few things in this life bequeath peace like a river. Isaiah the prophet knew it, for the Lord spoke to him on the subject. "For thus saith the Lord, Behold, I will extend peace to her like a river, and the glory of the Gentiles like a flowing stream." (66:12) "Peace like a river"—in their imagery, these are among the most inspired words of Scripture.

Four weeks I spent drifting down the Yukon river in a sixteen-foot rowboat, without benefit of motor, accompanied by a congenial friend and a little stove made out of a gasoline can. I wrote a story about it, in which these words appear:

"I wondered why people cared to travel the Yukon in anything so prosaic and unimaginative as a steamboat. They learned nothing of the ways of a river; they might as well have gone riding through the Royal Gorge in a boxcar. To live with it and on it, to drink of the body and spirit of the water, to become part of it, and to cherish the haunting beauty of the bend ahead, is to know a river. And when you do know it, then nothing else matters, for you have stolen a glimpse into the mystery of creation."

In the years since then I have come to know Jesus Christ to be my Savior and Lord, and I have discovered that His life too is like a river. It begins with a miracle, springing out of the watershed of life, coursing like a laughing brook down the early years. Then comes the sudden widening of the banks as the ministry of John the Baptist flows tributary into His stream, and the strong, impressive movement of the Galilean ministry begins.

Suddenly there is white water, and the first opposition is encountered. More riffles and rapids, and in between a swift, powerful flood bearing purposefully toward its destiny, carrying its appointed burden, spreading healing waters throughout the countryside until a roaring sound is heard in the distance. It is Passion Week. The dull sound now increases in intensity and the sheer cataract of the Cross is approached. Nearer and nearer the brink, and then—catastrophe!

But somehow it is not catastrophe at all, for there below is the river, newly formed, beginning a life of Resurrection that is majestic and serene as it flows to the seas of eternity.

The river is the symbol of God's purpose in your life and mine. It is never an end in itself because it has no real end except in the ocean of infinity. It is an instrument to carry out the balance of nature, as you and I are instruments to fulfill the design of our Lord. It is always in motion, always sweeping onward even when it seems to be quiescent, for its strength lies in its deep currents. Its bounty is in breadth but its resource is in depth.

The river's motion is the secret of its peace, for it portrays not the peace of man but the peace of God. The peace of man is the quiet pool which is dangerous, for such pools become stagnant and breed ill-health. The peace of man is lifeless; it is the peace of the tomb. The peace of God is gently moving, it is Jesus walking through the grain-fields of Galilee. But the gentleness may depart, and there will be white horses and water wheels, as when the tables were overturned in the temple. This too is the peace of God—"not as the world giveth, give I unto you."

Once we have learned the river's lesson, we are to leave it; for the river runs its own affairs and follows its vocation, as we are expected to find and follow ours. What is God's purpose for our lives? Is it not to make us fit for His own fellowship, and then to plant us in His vineyard to bear fruit? Is it not to call us to the mount of Transfiguration, and then send us back to look for fishermen who will leave their nets to catch men?

5

One of the most remarkable Christian statements of our generation was made by Professor Edmund Schlink of Heidelberg at the World Council of Churches meeting at Evanston in 1954. Said Dr. Schlink: [1]

We do not preach the Gospel in order that the world may be preserved. Rather we accept our responsibility for the preservation of the world in order that many may be saved through the Gospel. We do not preach the Gospel in order to bring about earthly justice. On the contrary we try to establish justice in order that we may preach the Gospel.

[1] Quoted in *Christian Century*, August 24, 1954, page 1010.

In four shocking sentences Dr. Schlink set forth the role of the Christian as a peacemaker in the world. He does not build and extend the Church in order to promote world peace. Instead he seeks a minimum of strife in order that he may build the Church. If not one blessing were to flow into this life from the Gospel, it would still be the Christian's commission to proclaim it, for the Gospel is the power of God unto salvation, and is therefore an end in itself.

If the Christian is lured into seeking the ideal of harmony and perfection among men, he is being false both to God and man. The Christian is a traveler passing through and seeking a better life. He looks upon this life as an adventure, a testing ground, a battlefield, and a recruiting depot. The adventures are soul-pioneering expeditions with God. The testings are the battles. They are struggles with the Power of Evil that make us more durable steel in the divine warhead.

But beyond all these, the Christian is called to be a vocational selector, searching for men who will receive the peace of the Kingdom of God. The recruiting of men of peace is what brings joy to the Christian, and it is this peace with joy that makes everything a Christian goes through ultimately worthwhile.

G. K. Chesterton once remarked that every real Christian who believes in his faith will do two things: he will dance, and he will fight. His fighting, however, is not against flesh and blood, and his joy according to the New Testament is more often linked with his peacemaking. Thus Paul writes to the Romans, "The kingdom of God is not meat and drink; but righteousness, and peace, and joy in the Holy Ghost." (14:17) When the apostles went through Judea and Samaria "preaching peace by Jesus Christ" we read that "there was great joy" in those regions. Peace and joy together appear as authentic marks of the Good News.

We have already suggested [2] that joy is not to be confused with pleasure or happiness, which are for many but fleeting experiences in life. Goethe at the age of seventy-five admitted that he had known only four weeks of happiness. There are Christians, victims of lifelong suffering, who could say the same thing. But joy! Here we move into a different dimension, and that telltale light comes into the eye of the believer. Joy is not happiness so much as gladness; it is the exultation of God's Spirit in man, "good measure, pressed down, and shaken together, and running over." Joy is the ecstasy of eternity in a soul that has made peace with God and is ready to do His will.

> Peace does not mean the end of all our striving,
> Joy does not mean the drying of our tears;
> Peace is the power that comes to souls arriving
> Up to the light where God Himself appears.
>
> —STUDDERT KENNEDY

When the Church of the twentieth century stands at the Great Assize it may not be judged for the shape of its liturgy, the heat of its ardor, or the sums of its stewardship. The Church will probably be judged be-

[2] Page 28.

cause it did not receive or make peace with joy. Visit a modern theological seminary, examine its library, and count the number of Christian volumes in which joy is never mentioned. "Peace on earth" was not a dogma, it was a song sung by angels. As Dorothy Sayers has said, the Church today has succeeded in doing what the apostles and even the enemies of Jesus Christ never did: it has made Him appear dull. What is the Church but the glowing hearth where man can warm his hands at the heart of God? What are its sacraments but a chalice of divine peace and joy?

We have assumed that Christianity is a tiresome and domesticated affair. Who made it so? I would prefer, like Wordsworth, to be a pagan lost forever in the superstitions of mythology than to return to the state of being of a bored "Christian." And though I do not care for violence, I would far rather have been at Calvary watching the wet, sticky blood flow down the Cross, hearing the raucous jeers of the crowd, smelling the stinks of Gehenna, and feeling the cool slime of the tomb, than to have to sit through the tedium of a joyless Sunday morning church service.

The resurrected Jesus came through the closed door and said "Peace!" to His disciples, but it was a peace amid clamor and tumult. It was the peace of life and joy, not the peace of tranquilizers and sanitariums. Such was the kind of life Jesus led, and such is the only kind of peace He gives. We can have it anywhere, any time, simply for the asking. God built it into the poles and axles of the universe.

BLESSED ARE THEY WIIICII ARE PERSECUTED FOR
RIGHTEOUSNESS' SAKE: FOR THEIRS IS THE KINGDOM
OF HEAVEN.

8

Christian Courage

I

PERSECUTED?

A strange word, and rather unseemly. Are we then
to go about seeking someone to badger and bedevil us
that we might be "blessed"?

Let us imagine that our pilgrimage has brought us
through the very gates of Jerusalem, and it is the week
of the Passover feast. Jesus of Nazareth, who spoke this
Beatitude on a northerly mountain, is today preparing
for His final ordeal, an ordeal of persecution. Our eighth
Beatitude quite evidently is more than a simple Galilean
proverb; it is a prediction of the sufferings of the Messiah. Like the seven signal flares sent up before it, the
Beatitude lights the way to the Cross of Calvary.

In some ways the New Testament is a handbook for

the persecuted. It was written to give courage and fortitude to those who were about to be brainwashed. That is why reading the Bible is such an unreal experience for many Americans, and it is why in Korea today Christians are rising at forty-thirty o'clock for prayer and study. Our trouble is not with the King James Version, for that version, like the original New Testament, was written in a day of persecution—the ashes of Smithfield were still hot—and it carries the wild, authentic note of the early Church. Our trouble is with us: we are too accommodating about our faith. We are tolerated rather than persecuted, and our gospel is tame and stifled. The new translations show it; they are so often "sicklied o'er with the pale cast of thought."

In the original autographs every gospel, every letter carries the message, "Stand fast in your trial. Take heart. Play the man. Be valiant in the faith." The New Testament is the manual of prescribed reading in that extra-curricular course, Martyrdom 1-A.

So it is that our Beatitude is cast in steel. It inters forever the woebegone hope that somehow man is going to solve all his troubles so that our grandchildren will grow up "in clover." It pours scorn upon those who yearn for a life of ease. "Thou therefore endure hardness, as a good soldier of Jesus Christ." (II Timothy 2:3) The Word is: be meek, aye, be merciful, but be tough.

In the New Testament two kinds of suffering are to be distinguished. There is that pain and invalidism which Jesus Christ identified as the work of Satan, and from which He rescued and healed all who sought His path. There was also the suffering of persecution, to which He invited His followers with a kind of holy joy that even today makes the spine tingle. Jesus promised adventure—and risk—but never uncertainty. He said the Christian's persecution was certain; the only variable element was the way in which it would come.

Our Lord said further that our persecution would prove to be a blessing. Blessings come from God. In His will and for His purpose God deliberately metes out to His own this kind of suffering. So determined is our Lord that we shall be trained and hardened for His work, that He sends us test after test in a lifelong spiritual fitness program.

> My son, despise not thou the chastening [discipline] of the Lord, nor faint when thou art rebuked of him: For whom the Lord loveth he chasteneth, and scourgeth every son whom he receiveth.
>
> If ye endure chastening, God dealeth with you as with sons; for what son is he whom the father chasteneth not? But if ye be without chastisement, whereof all are partakers, then are ye bastards, and not sons. (Hebrews 12:5–8)

The deeper a believer gets into God's training program, the more he realizes that God will stop at nothing to bring one of his sons or daughters to proper conditioning. It may even seem that God is reckless in the way He exposes us to the perils of the world, but He always knows what He is doing. He "will not suffer you to be tempted above that ye are able." (I Corinthians 10:13) Furthermore, He expects us not to weep and shake our heads about our situation, but to *revel* in it.

> My brethren, count it all joy when ye fall into divers temptations; knowing this, that the trying of your faith worketh patience. But let patience have her perfect work, that ye may be perfect and entire. . . . (James 1:2–4)
>
> We glory in tribulations . . . knowing that tribulation worketh patience; and patience, experience; and experience, hope. (Romans 5:3–4)

Hannah Whitall Smith illustrates the purpose of God by proposing to describe to a stranger—say a visitor from another planet—the way in which a lump of clay is made into a beautiful vessel: [1]

> I tell him first the part of the clay in the matter; and all I can say about this is, that the clay is put into the potter's hands, and then lies passive there, submitting itself to all the turnings and overturnings of the potter's hands upon it. There is really nothing else to be said about the clay's part.

Then she traces the role that the potter plays in the process:

> The potter takes the clay thus abandoned to his working, and begins to mold and fashion it according to his own will. He kneads and works it; he tears it apart and presses it together again; he wets it and then suffers

[1] *The Christian's Secret of a Happy Life*, Fleming H. Revell Company, 1883.

114

it to dry. Sometimes he works at it for hours together; sometimes he lays it aside for days, and does not touch it. And when . . . he has made it perfectly pliable in his hands, he proceeds to make it into the vessel he has proposed. He turns it upon the wheel, planes it and smooths it, and dries it in the sun, bakes it in the oven, and finally turns it out of his workshop, a vessel to his honor, and fit for his use.

2

The Church may be entering a new era of persecution in the will of God. If so, that is good news according to our Beatitude. No one will deny that in recent years the signs have been increasing. Pressures in Germany, in the Middle East, in Korea, in China, in parts of Africa may well be heralds of something more formidable. It is idle to speculate, but the Church of Jesus Christ would be wise in these days to take stock of its supply of courage.

What is courage? What is its anatomy? Can we reduce it to a compound of self-centered motives, such as the fear of extermination, resentment over ridicule, desire to dominate, longing for social approval, sheer bravado or the unconscious death-wish?

What makes a man behave bravely?

If we look in the New Testament we find the word "courage" mentioned only once. When Paul was being delivered to Rome as a prisoner, Luke says that some of the Christian brethren came to greet him at the Appii Forum on the outskirts of the city, "whom when Paul saw, he thanked God, and took courage." (Acts 28:15)

There were no "brethren" about to encourage the Lord Jesus Christ as He faced His accusers at the last. Maundy Thursday was not the disciples' "finest hour." They worked up an argument at the supper table. They went to sleep in the prayer meeting, and they panicked in the face of the mob. They fled from Jesus as rats deserting a sinking ship. In the language of our day it could be said that one of Christ's disciples "turned Him in," another "dummied up," and the rest "bugged out."

Yet within a few weeks these same disciples were showing a kind of valor and courage in the face of persecution that steeled them through one ordeal after another, and has continued to amaze the world for two thousand years. How was it possible? What was their secret?

There is an interesting phrase connected with all the accounts of the Last Supper on that Thursday night: *"When he had given thanks."* Paul, you will remember, received courage as he thanked God. He took his courage not only from the brethren but from the Lord. He gave thanks for the situation in which he found himself, and courage was given. Is that what Jesus did on the night of His betrayal? It is an action so simple that the world overlooks it as "obvious," but it is loaded with power. Whenever Christians start thanking God in tight situations, look for courage to be shown.

General Harrison, who signed the Panmunjom truce for the United States and was later stationed in the Canal Zone, supervised the removal of the bodies of five young American missionary martyrs who were slaughtered by the Auca Indians of the Amazon jungle early in 1956.

Bill Carle, the singer, visited the general shortly afterward, and quoted him as saying that in his military experience he had never seen courage like that displayed by the five dedicated young women who were made widows by the tragedy. What was the source of their courage? The answer is not hard to find. Lovers of Jesus Christ have always counted it a privilege to be allowed to suffer on His account.

Thus James Guthrie, on the morning of his execution in Tolbooth prison, declared after the Psalmist, "This is the day which the Lord hath made; we will rejoice and be glad in it." (118:24) Persecution drove the Pilgrim Fathers out of Europe, and the Pilgrim Fathers in return gave us Thanksgiving Day. Their remarks on the subject of courage are worth repeating. William Bradford, one of their leaders, described the *Mayflower* voyage in these words: [2]

> All great and honourable actions are accompanied with great difficulties, and must be enterprised and overcome with answerable courages. It was granted the dangers were great, but not desperate; the difficulties were many, but not invincible . . . and all of them, through the help of God, by fortitude and patience, might either be borne, or overcome. . . . Yea, though they should loose their lives in this action, yet might they have comforte in the same. . . .

Sanna M. Barlow, in her account of recent missionary activity among the Kikuyu tribesmen of Kenya, East Africa, tells how some of the African Christians

[2] *History of Plymouth Plantation* (W. T. Davis, ed.), Charles Scribner's Sons, New York, 1908, page 46.

117

"speak of our Brother Stephen as though he, the first Christian martyr, lived only yesterday." [3] Primitive though they may be, they came through the Mau Mau terrors with a faith triumphant and authentic, as they declared it an honor to have their coffee trees destroyed for the name of Jesus Christ. Geoffrey Bull proved in a Chinese prison that Christian courage stands even the test of Communist brainwashing when built upon the rock of Christ.[4] Yet in a sense such courage is not given; it is only lent by God to those whom He loves, that in time of trouble they might overcome persecution for righteousness' sake.

Whatever may be the anatomy of other kinds of courage, the Christian kind is based only upon the weakness of the human flesh and the power of the Holy Spirit.

3

One of the events in American history we would like to forget is the hanging of the Salem "witches." Many of the most distinguished men of the commonwealth of Massachusetts were caught up in the hysteria that swept the colony in 1692. Among those who later confessed their error in taking part in the trials, there was a well-known Boston lawyer, Judge Samuel Sewall, who walked with God in the matter.

For the rest of his life Samuel Sewall was a different man. He declared publicly that he was chiefly responsi-

[3] *Light Is Sown*, Moody Press, Chicago, 1956.
[4] *When Iron Gates Yield*, Moody Press, Chicago, 1956.

ble for the travesty, and desired "to take the blame and shame of it, asking pardon of men." Every year he set one day aside on the anniversary of his public repentance, doing no work, eating no food, but praying and reflecting upon his "guilt contracted at Salem."

You and I have walked with Jesus together through these pages. We now stand outside the city gates at the trail's end, the Place of the Skull. We have learned many things as we walked with Him, and we shall not be quite the same again, for we know now that our own crucifixion is involved. That is what Jesus wanted. He never intended Calvary to become simply a memorial to Himself. The Shepherd's thought is for the sheep. His wish was that His disciples would reflect upon their own lives, now nailed with His to the Cross. Good Friday is recapitulated in every Christian's heart. We are the ones who stand before Pilate and witness to the truth. We are the scorned, the slapped, the flogged, the persecuted. We lift a cross to our bleeding shoulders; we wear the crown of thorns, we feel the blows of the hammer and the prick of the spear through our flesh. As He was in this life, so are we: reckoned dead to this world and its sin, that we might be alive to God through Jesus Christ.

A young man whose father had recently passed away came before the session of my Church to present himself as a candidate for communicant membership. He was duly asked his reasons therefor, and replied, "Well, the old man is dead!" Some of the elders were mystified as to what he meant, not realizing that he was speaking of his own Christian experience; but the Scriptures upheld the young man: "Our old man is crucified with him, that the body of sin might be destroyed, that henceforth we should not serve sin. For . . . if we be dead with Christ, we believe that we shall also live with him." (Romans 6:6–8)

King Clovis of Gaul, who was "converted" to Christianity and who had a habit of lopping off the heads of all who refused to follow his example, once boasted that if his invincible Franks had been at Golgotha, they would have risen to the defense and rescue of Jesus. How easy it is to miss the meaning of the atonement! The New Testament was not written to describe "the day Christ died," but rather to make each of us a witness to "the day I died."

It is well for us to remember today not only the persecution of our Lord, but to join with Judge Sewall in looking over the past that is our personal history. Did we take care of those spiritual matters that we promised to see to? Have we spoken that reconciling word that we intended to utter, but keep forgetting? Is there yet unfinished restitution that keeps us from burying the past as it should be buried?

Let us be very sure that our old natures are not still hanging on the Cross. Let us not seek to cling to a spark of life, but rather say with our Lord, "It is finished. Father, into thy hands I commend my spirit."

> O Cross that liftest up my head,
>   I dare not ask to fly from Thee;
> I lay in dust, life's glory, dead,

And from the ground there blossoms red
Life that shall endless be.

4

What is persecution?

So twisted are the values we set on things that the
very word is suspect. Its meaning hangs in doubt. What
may appear to the sufferer as persecution often turns out
to be a mild (or not so mild) form of persecutory
paranoia. At the same time what is being palmed off to
one-third of the world's population as "re-education"
according to Marx turns out to be the deadliest form of
persecution that the Church has ever encountered.

Our Beatitude has frequently been misinterpreted
and has even been used to aggravate a mental condition.
Thus there are people who have taken the words of Jesus
to be a confirmation of their suspicions that they are the
victims of persecution. They are satisfied that the world
is against them just because they have taken a stand "for
righteousness' sake." For them it is "God and I" ranged
against the forces of darkness; or, as in many modern
cases (as with Hitler) it may be simply "My Battle."

The world knows few types more dangerous than
the man deluded by a persecution complex. Once convinced that "they're out to get me," he may give himself
over to retaliation that is merciless. His days and nights
are then passed in the fashioning of cunning and savage
plans against his "enemies." The deterioration of a personality in the grip of paranoia is a fearful thing to watch.
Hatcher Hughes, in his play *Hell Bent fer Heaven*,

portrays a Carolina hillbilly "talking to his Lord" in the midst of a feud: [5]

They wuz a time, Lord, when my proud heart said, "All o' self an' none o' Thee." Then You come a-knockin' at the door o' my sinful soul an' I whispered, "Some o' self an' some o' Thee." But that's all changed now, Lord. I'm Yourn an' You are mine. An' the burden o' my song now is, "None o' self an' all o' Thee." You can do with me what You please, Lord. If it's Your will that this blasphemer shall die, I've got a whole box of dynamite out in the store . . . I can blow up the dam while he's under thar a-telephonin', an' the waters o' Your wrath'll sweep over him like they did over Pharaoh. . . .

On the other hand there is a persecution that is quite real. It is found in the New Testament and its heavy hand has been felt by the Church many times since. To the Roman emperors it was simply a matter of civil administration. The little sect of Christians refused to conform, therefore it was outlawed and scattered. Ancient Rome by and large was completely bored with the claims of the early Church; like Gallio, Rome "cared for none of those things." (Acts 18:17) She swatted the Christians as one would swat a pesky fly.

In the twentieth century a new persecution of the Church has arisen, so subtle that it does not appear to a large section of the Church to be a persecution at all. The cadres and commissars behind the Iron Curtain who are assigned the task of indoctrinating the masses

[5] New York, Harper and Brothers, 1924. Quoted by permission.

122

away from their faith were not born yesterday. They know that "the blood of the martyrs is the seed of the Church." Wherever possible they have sought to avoid the stigma of direct persecution. Their purpose is not so much to root out or extirpate the faithful Christians as it is to launder their ideas. Thus those who have spent time in Communist labor camps and prisons tell how the discussion method is used to bring about "acceptable" points of view. Endless conversations are carried on, day after day, until the mind is worn to a stupor, and almost any proposition seems credible enough to elicit a convincing response. No lions, no gladiators, no libations on the altar of Diana are as terrifying to face as the dreary brainwashing of the discussion. The wheel comes full circle as Marxism is made the opium of the people.

Our day has known its share of both these types: the man who imagines he is persecuted and is not, and the man who imagines he is not persecuting, but is. And in the center is the Church of Jesus Christ, girding its loins for its latest ordeal, seeking fidelity to truth as it confronts as menacing a challenge as it has ever faced.

There is nothing imaginary about the threat! When Karl Marx was a seventeen-year-old schoolboy at a Lutheran preparatory school in western Germany, he wrote a lovely essay on John 15, "I am the Vine"; but within a few years he was prefacing his doctor's thesis with a quotation from Prometheus, "I hate all the gods!"; and today his hatred has been fanned into a flame that threatens to sweep the planet. Demolition crews stand ready, awaiting the signal to cut down the cathedrals, save where it is expedient that they should first become museums.

What is God's message to His people thus caught in the modern counter-currents of simulation and dissimulation? We are told to be calm, to be at peace, in fact, to rejoice and be glad. Whatever may come, all is well. The faith is in good hands. The Kingdom of God is nigh. In the days that lie ahead the Church's persecutions may become even more artful and diabolical, but it will survive them too. It cannot help surviving. Even if Communism should capture the wavering population of the globe, and set up its Pilate and its Caiaphas who, in the name of "freedom of religion," would condemn the Church of Jesus Christ to the Cross, it does not matter. The Church belongs at the Cross. That is the only place where it will ever find Victory and Resurrection. That is the only place where the world has ever discovered the true significance of the Gospel. (Mark 15:39)

Blessed are the persecuted, for their message is authentic. Their sufferings are their credentials. "From henceforth let no man trouble me:" wrote Paul, "for I bear in my body the marks of the Lord Jesus." (Galatians 6:17) Let there be no doubt that the God who made history will save His people in the midst of history. Their tribulations will only hasten the great Day of the Church. "God is in the midst of her; she shall not be moved: God shall help her, and that right early." (Psalm 46:5) Blessed are the persecuted, for in the fire they are purified; yet when fire comes, we must be girt and ready.

God grant that we who are His Church may be wise enough to tell the real from the false, and to stand fast in the truth.

5

The rock . . .
The Roman lock . . .
What is there to it?
How did he do it?

They tell me he is risen
Out of death's prison
But how can that be?
What did they see?

O terror of that daybreak hour
O rapture of the Savior's power,
O Life that broke but did not bend,
O grave that burst from end to end!

You are a temple guard in Jerusalem. You have been losing sleep for some days. There was the affair Thursday night—the arrest, the questioning, and general disorder. Friday night you were assigned to guard a tomb in the garden of Joseph of Arimathaea, and you are still there. It is now early Sunday morning, and you have settled back against a nearby rock to steal forty winks. You have a dream: a mighty angel appears before you with feet widespread. He raises his arm and places a golden trumpet to his lips, and there issues forth a blast that shatters the air and causes the earth beneath you to tremble. You waken in a sweat, fearing the end of everything. All is quiet; your comrades are drowsing. Then you peer through the gray murk at the tomb that is your responsibility. Something about it seems to be different. You rub your eyes, get up, and walk toward it, only to stop amazed at the sight of the broken seal. The stone has been rolled aside. For a moment you are shocked into rigidity. Then you shout, you summon the guard, and there ensues—pandemonium!

You have been the first to witness the power of the Resurrection.

"The Gospels," says John S. Whale, "cannot explain the Resurrection; it is the Resurrection which alone explains the Gospels. The Resurrection is not an appendage to the Christian faith; it is the Christian faith." [6]

The disciples heard Jesus Christ tell of His approaching persecution and describe it as the will of God. They heard His word concerning their own persecutions which were to follow: "Blessed are ye, when men shall revile you, and persecute you, and shall say all manner of evil against you falsely, for my sake. Rejoice, and be exceeding glad: for great is your reward in heaven: for so persecuted they the prophets which were before you." (Matthew 5:11–12) Somehow they never added two and two together until the two sprinters, John and Peter, stood breathless before the eerie wonder of the empty cave. It took the Resurrection to put a heartbeat into the embryo Church and bring it to life. *He is not here, for He is risen!*

Did it happen?

[6] *Christian Doctrine,* The Macmillan Company, New York, 1942.

Johannes Weiss says the Resurrection appearances were an optical illusion. Many claim that the disciples only "thought they saw Jesus" and "felt He was near." Such theories do not solve our problem, however; they complicate it, for they make it more difficult than ever to interpret the power of the early Christians, or to explain how the persecuted can be blessed. Let us join the theorists for a moment and look at the Cross from their vantage point. What do we see?

We see a rubbish heap outside Jerusalem, where a mob of soldiers and onlookers is gathered, howling for blood. We see three dead men nailed to gibbets, the carrion birds beginning to circle, the hounds skulking in the background and waiting for their chance after nightfall. We see the final frustration of the Messiah, the Christ, the noblest soul the world has ever known, apparently terribly mistaken in His claims of Deity. And we find ourselves saying that there is no God, at least there is no God who can really be said to care for men. And if God does not care, then why should we care? We can turn our eyes away from the crosses and look elsewhere, but there seem to be only more crosses. "If in this life only we have hope in Christ, we are of all men most miserable. . . ."

But now is Christ RISEN!

Risen! Not a fancy but a fact. Not a violation of natural law but the fulfillment of a supernatural law. "Whom God hath raised up, having loosed the pains of death: because it was not possible that he should be holden of it." (Acts 2:24) As Leith Samuel says, Jesus

Christ was the Eternal Son, the Co-Creator and Redeemer of the universe. Death had no claim upon Him because He had never sinned. And when He covered our sins at Calvary, He also covered our death, our mortality.

The reality of Easter is founded upon the reality of the Cross. Men will continue to suggest that Easter is not really a miracle; that it is rather a kind of seasonal vitamin tablet or spiritual shot in the arm for the lifting of flagging spirits and the assuaging of cultural dislocations. Easter, however, points back to the Cross. And on the Cross we are ourselves *crucified* with Jesus Christ to the world; we become spiritually *dead* in order that He might live in us as Christus Victor, King of Kings and Lord of Lords.

Thus the persecuted ones find themselves keeping company with all the heroes of the faith; with Moses at the Red Sea, and David in the cave of Adullam, and Paul and Silas in the jail at Philippi, and Bull in Chungking, and Bonhoeffer in Germany, and the pastor martyrs in Korea, and the Christian Kikuyus in Kenya. But they also find themselves with the poor in spirit, with the mourners, with the meek, the hungry and thirsty, the merciful, the pure in heart, and the peacemakers. And they find themselves with Job, stripped of everything but God, and yet blessed: ". . . as dying, and, behold, we live; as chastened, and not killed; as sorrowful, yet alway rejoicing; as poor, yet making many rich; as having nothing, and yet possessing all things." (II Corinthians 6:9–10)

Our Beatitudes close with the promise of the Kingdom of Heaven and the exhortation to rejoice in gladness. Our journey has ended on a triumphant note of Resurrection joy. What we have lost, we have been given back in double measure, an Easter gift for eternity, and our cups are running over.

All which I took from thee I did but take,
  Not for thy harms,
But just that thou might'st seek it in My arms.

—FRANCIS THOMPSON